Endometriosis

Don't Let It Take Over Your Life

By: Barton Press

Copyright © 2021 by Barton Press

ALL RIGHTS RESERVED

No part of this book may be reproduced, stored in a retrieval system, or transmitted in any form or by any means, electronic, mechanical, photocopying, recording, scanning, or otherwise, without the prior written permission of the publisher.

Limit of Liability/Disclaimer of Warranty: the publisher and the author make no representations or warranties with respect to the accuracy or completeness of the contents of this work and specifically disclaim all warranties, including without limitation warranties of fitness for a particular purpose. No warranty may be created or extended by sales or promotional materials. The advice and strategies contained herein may not be suitable for every situation. This work is sold with the understanding that the publisher is not engaged in rendering medical, legal or other professional advice or services. If professional assistance is required, the services of a competent professional person should be sought. Neither the publisher nor the author shall be liable for damages arising herefrom. The fact that an individual, organization or website is referred to in this work as a citation and/or potential source of further information does not mean that the author or the publisher endorses the information the individuals, organization or website may provide or recommendations they/it may make. Further, readers should be aware that websites listed on this work may have changed or disappeared between when this work was written and when it is read.

Medical Disclaimer: This booklet is based on personal research and is intended as a general guide to help those suffering from Endometriosis who would prefer to take a more natural approach to their treatment. It is not a substitute for the advice of a medical professional. Readers are advised to always consult their personal physician before implementing any changes to their medical care.

Contents

Part One: What is Endometriosis? 1

Introduction to Endometriosis: 1

Disorder Symptoms: 3

Potential Cause and Diagnosis: 8

"Traditional Treatment" 20

Part Two: Endometriosis and Holistic Medicine 25

Steps to Holistic Healing: 25

Diet and Endometriosis 27

Deficiencies and supplements: 50

Herbal Remedies: 60

Exercise and Endometriosis: 69

Part Three: Cultivating a better life with endometriosis 76

Lifestyle changes: 76

Avoiding Environmental Toxins: 91

Therapies and Treatments: 103

Emotional Healing: 140

Summary: 162

Citations 171

Part One: What is Endometriosis?

Introduction to Endometriosis:

Endometriosis is a chronic disease caused by the abnormal growth of endometrial tissue (the tissue that normally lines the uterus) outside of the uterus. When this occurs, the tissue can spread to the ovaries, fallopian tubes, and even the intestines. The condition can cause debilitating pain, infertility, and a general decrease in quality of life. Some women have described endometriosis pain as burning like an electric shock, similar to contractions while giving birth, or even like being stabbed repeatedly in the abdomen.

Women with endometriosis oftentimes feel like their life is put on hold during their menstrual cycle. Debilitating pain, heavy bleeding, nausea, vomiting, diarrhea, and other symptoms can make day-to-day activities next to impossible.

While pain from endometriosis is frequently at its worst during the menstrual cycle, it is not confined to it. Severe pelvic pain, cramping, fatigue, gastrointestinal problems, and even bleeding might appear at any time of the month. When endometriosis spreads to the ovaries it can often result in recurring ovarian cysts, which can rupture and cause irreparable damage.

To the outside world, a woman with endometriosis might appear completely fine on a good day, but it can damage almost every aspect of a woman's life. Endometriosis can affect a woman's ability to work, exercise, and have children. It can result in painful sex, interrupt one's ability to socialize, or interfere with carrying out simple daily tasks. Many women with endometriosis suffer from depression and other mood disorders, both due to hormone imbalances, and the psychological toll of living with chronic pain. Women with endometriosis can often feel like they are missing out on life. It can seem like fighting an invisible battle with your own body that your friends and family cannot begin to understand.

Estimates suggest that at least 10% of all premenopausal women are affected by endometriosis, which is equivalent to almost 200 million women worldwide.[1] However, despite its prevalence, endometriosis remains tragically misunderstood and research is scarce; leading many who suffer from it to feel isolated and alone.

Endometriosis is often misdiagnosed or undiagnosed, sometimes for years. Women who suffer from endometriosis can often feel like the pain they suffer is not taken seriously. Sadly, this has historically been true in many cases. Many women who grow up with endometriosis are led to believe that the excruciating, debilitating pain they feel, is a normal aspect of being a woman. They might even be told they are being "overdramatic" when they try to articulate their pain.

Thankfully, as taboos around talking about female health and reproductive disorders have begun to fade, many women are becoming more open about their struggles with endometriosis.

If you are reading this guide it is likely that you or someone you know is affected by endometriosis. You might feel discouraged or even hopeless by a lack of options for dealing with your condition. You might have been let down by conventional medicine in the past. The goal of this guide is to provide some options and answers for those suffering from endometriosis that may not be found elsewhere. The journey to healing can be a difficult one, but it is possible.

Disorder Symptoms:

Endometriosis is characterized by the growth of endometrial tissue outside of the lining of the uterus. In the average healthy woman, with a normally functioning reproductive system, the endometrial tissue will break down every month and be shed during the menstrual period. Hormones known as prostaglandins facilitate this process. Prostaglandins are the same hormones that are released by the body at the site of an injury to encourage clotting, by inducing an inflammatory response. Acute or short term inflammation can actually be beneficial, and even necessary to the bodies healing process. [2] However, when inflammation becomes excessive and constant, it can become harmful.

In the uterus, prostaglandins act to cause contractions. This can be either the contractions during labor, or the monthly contractions to shed the endometrial lining during the menstrual period. Because of the contractions and inflammation caused by the prostaglandins many women, even those without endometriosis, will experience mild cramping, loose stools, and nausea with their menstrual cycle. [3] The higher the amounts of prostaglandins produced by a woman's body, the more likely she is to experience more severe cramping and other symptoms.

In women with endometriosis the endometrial tissue commonly spreads to the ovaries, bowels, and pelvic tissue, but can also spread further. In fact, in rare cases, endometriosis has been found in almost all body tissues and organs in the lower body, excluding the spleen. [4] The spread of endometrial tissue into other parts of the abdomen prevents it from exiting the body as it would during a normal menstrual period. This results in higher levels of inflammation, and much more severe pain and cramping.

This **intense pelvic pain** during the menstrual period is the primary symptom of endometriosis. The severe pelvic pain and cramping that women with endometriosis experience during their menstrual periods can extend to the lower back, abdomen, pubic symphysis, inside the vaginal canal, and even the legs. Pain during ovulation, known as Mittelschmerz, is also common.

Abnormally heavy bleeding during the menstrual period, as well as **thick clotting,** is also common in women with endometriosis. This can lead to those with the disorder being more at risk for anemia, due to losing an increased amount of blood/iron in the menstrual blood. Spotting and abnormal bleeding outside of the menstrual period is also common. **Irregular menstrual periods** are also common.

Bowel and urinary problems are also common in those affected by endometriosis. Painful bowel movements and urination are especially common during the menstrual period but can also occur at any point in the cycle. Many women with endometriosis have persistent irritable bowel syndrome, resulting in bouts of both constipation and diarrhea. Many also experience severe nausea, especially during the menstrual period.

Physical signs of endometriosis often manifest in **ovarian cysts** and **adhesions**. Ovarian cysts are small fluid-filled cysts in the ovarian tissue that can grow, and eventually rupture. When a cyst ruptures, the fluid inside spreads throughout the abdominal cavity; which can cause excruciating pain. Adhesions are scar tissue that form between organs causing them to essentially stick together. This can also cause significant pain. While both cysts and adhesions can be treated by surgery, they frequently come back; and sometimes surgical scar tissues can lead to developing even more adhesions.

Inability to enjoy sexual intercourse or painful sexual intercourse is also commonly reported in women with endometriosis. Women with endometriosis may not be able to have pleasurable sexual intercourse and may experience severe pain with vaginal penetration. Pain may linger after having sex, and some might experience spotting afterwards as well.

Another serious effect of endometriosis can be **fertility problems**. Many women with endometriosis have problems conceiving and carrying a baby to term. Some can even become infertile due to damage caused to the reproductive organs by the disease.

Many women living with endometriosis, also struggle with **psychological disease**. Anxiety, depression, and other mental health problems are common. Women with endometriosis on average show higher levels of introversion, anger, anxiety, and depressive thoughts. These symptoms are all concurrent with limited social availability, loss of working ability, dissatisfaction with work and family life, and a general decrease in quality of life. [5]

Studies have also shown that women with endometriosis are more likely to exhibit somatization —the manifestation of physical symptoms due to emotional distress.[5] This occurs as a result of the mind-body connection which our bodies originally evolved in order to protect us from danger. For example, if you feel afraid your "fight or flight" responses might kick into gear— increased heart rate, tense muscles, hypervigilance. These responses are innate and involuntary, and they are excellent at preparing us to survive an attack from a predator. However, when you are being faced with a trip to the grocery store for example, and not an attack from a sabretooth tiger, this physiological response is not so helpful.

The stress caused by the chronic pain can lead to a somatic response. This somatic response can in turn cause increased endometriosis pain, which then in turn increases stress levels.

This perpetuates a vicious cycle of increasing stress and pain, which wears down both the body and the mind. [5]

Studies have also showed that persistent painful stimuli, such as the chronic pelvic pain experienced by women with endometriosis, over time can lead to increased awareness of pain. Essentially, the longer one suffers with the disease, the more heightening the body's response becomes, and the more intense the pain feels. [6]

Not everyone with endometriosis will have all these symptoms and having these symptoms does not necessarily indicate a diagnosis of endometriosis. There are other reproductive health conditions that may cause similar problems. However, if you are experiencing some or all of them, it may be a strong indicator that you are one of the many women world-wide that suffers from endometriosis.

Potential Cause and Diagnosis:

Unfortunately, a definitive answer for the cause of endometriosis is unknown. Much research is still left to be done to identify the cause and potential "cure." Here we will go over some of the theories that have been proposed to explain the occurrence of the disease.

Historical Theories:

The first known references to a painful menstruation disorder which could have been endometriosis are found in the Ebers Papyrus, a document from 1500 B.C. Egypt. The Ebers Papyrus was a medical papyrus that contained information on herbal treatments for a variety of different conditions. This abnormality was attributed to "a scrape of the uterus" and either Nile mud mixed with honey and galena, a dressing of chopped onions, or mash and pine sawdust was the prescribed treatment. [7]

Ancient Greco-Roman physicians were familiar with gynecological issues such as endometriosis, as seen in many works from classical and late antiquity. Such problems were attributed to a "wandering womb" — an unfortunate side effect of a woman failing to meet her social duty of motherhood. The Greek Hippocratic texts, known as the Hippocratic Corpus, were a compilation of works written by various Greek medical professionals throughout the 4th and 5th centuries BC. These texts offer detailed reports of menstrual disorders. "Grumulous clots" that sometimes appeared as "black blood, resembling flesh" and "ulcers, inflammation of the uterus, pain, erratic fever, chills, nausea, and heartburn" were all noted as symptoms. They stated however, that this was "more commonly... the case with virgins than with married women" and therefore concluded that the best solution was to suppress symptoms via pregnancy.[8]

The Romans referred to the disease as "the suffocation of the womb." Claudius Galen of Pergamon, a Roman physician who lived from 129–216 AD, suggested that suffocation of the womb was caused by the membranes that anchor the uterus in place becoming engorged as from an excess of menstrual blood. This description is not too far from our modern understanding of adhesions and ligaments that are infiltrated by endometrial tissue. Galen noted that this caused "violent and painful uterine contractions." He was also one of the first to acknowledge the tie between endometriosis and mental illness, observing that young women with the condition were sometimes "driven to madness." [8]

During the Middle Ages in Europe, a time colloquially known as "The Dark Ages," much medical and scientific progress seemed to come to an abrupt halt. As European countries were plagued by societal unrest, wars, and pestilence, many turned to theological and supernatural explanations for sickness. Illness was frequently associated with sin or demonic possession, and it was not uncommon for some amount of blame to be placed on the sufferer. "Suffocation of the womb" came to be associated with "impure" women, or women that used herbal contraception, something that was heavily frowned upon. As attitudes became harsher so did treatments. Shouting at, or choking the necks of women, with "suffocation of the womb" were both presented as valid courses of action.

While progress might have been sidelined in Europe during this time, that was not the case in other parts of the world. In ancient Chinese Medicine the blame for endometriosis was not placed on the sufferer, but on "blood stasis" which was thought to be a result of a "stagnant energy" restricting blood circulation and affecting metabolism. Therefore, common treatments were herbs to vitalize blood circulation and acupuncture to relieve pain and correct energy imbalances. Pomegranates, which are now known to contain high levels of antioxidants and have anti-inflammatory properties, were also commonly prescribed. Other traditional Chinese medicines have been found to be anti-inflammatory as well. [8]

While the Renaissance of the 16th century and the subsequent 17th century showed overall scientific and medical improvement for Europe, treatment of women's health still took several steps backward. Demonic possession, witchcraft, hysteria, and nymphomania were all common blames. These ideas paved the way for the dismissal of endometriosis and other reproductive conditions as "psychological" for years to come. [8]

One exception to this prevailing ideology was the German physician Daniel Shrön. In 1690 he was the first to describe in detail the physical effects of endometriosis on the uterus. His work was pioneering in a time when microscopes were still incredibly rudimentary. In fact, he carried out many of his observations with a powerful magnifying glass. Shrön identified the various types of tissue in the uterus, and noted abnormalities, such as swelling, ulcers, and lesions. He proposed that these abnormalities were due to either refluxed or stagnated blood. Shrön was also, however, one of the first to recognize a potentially hereditary component to endometriosis. "There are certain families in whom ulcers erupt as though it were by hereditary right, and others also have observed the same phenomenon," he said. [8]

Unfortunately, Shrön's objective and scientific attitude towards endometriosis did not persist in society as a whole. For the next few centuries, many doctors and scientists still fell back on the "psychological" theory. Finally, in 1860, the microscopic discovery of endometriosis was achieved by Austrian pathologist Karl von Rokitansky. He was the first to identify what he called "cystosarcomas", what is now referred to as adenomyosis —when the endometrial tissue grows into the muscle wall of the uterus. However, despite his remarkable pathological identifications, he did not necessarily make the connection to symptoms of endometriosis, and his work went mostly unreferenced by other doctors investigating the disease.

Of all the scientists in the 1800's, it was Thomas Cullen, the man responsible for establishing the first gynecologic pathology laboratory at Johns Hopkins Hospital, who made some of the most significant progress in the field. He realized that uterine adenomyosis was always traced to the endometrium, a discovery that disproved previous theories that it might have been originating in the stomach tissue. Cullen also discovered that endometriosis could spread to the pelvic nerves, explaining some of the severe pain patients felt. He also reported kidney damage and endometriosis-related bowel obstruction. [8]

By the 1940s, endometriosis had been discovered everywhere from the cervix and bladder, to the colon, lymph nodes, and even lungs. More cases in younger patients, including teenage girls, also began to be recognized. During this time-period, scientists also began to realize the connection between endometriosis and hormone irregularities. The development of artificial hormones was relatively recent, and they began to be used as potential treatments.[8]

In the latter half of the 20th century, routine checkups and therefore treatment, for female reproductive health conditions, became more common. Hormonal contraceptives began to be prescribed, though the early pills had many negative side effects. Surgery, both laparotomies and hysterectomies, became common practice. [8]

Modern Theories:

In modern times, while we certainly know much more about endometriosis than a thousand years ago, we still know shockingly little when compared with other diseases. A definitive cause is unknown. One of the oldest theories, which is still prominent today, is that endometriosis is caused by **retrograde menstruation**. Retrograde menstruation is backwards flow of menstrual blood up through the fallopian tubes into the pelvic cavity. The theory proposes that the menstrual blood takes with it endometrial cells, that can then implant in the pelvic cavity and cause endometrial lesions. [9]

Stem cell theory proposes that stem cells, not the endometrial cells themselves are responsible for the growth of the endometrial tissues outside the uterus. Stem cells are responsible for regeneration. When in the correct location, the uterus, they cause the endometrial lining to regenerate after a menstrual cycle. However, if these cells were to be outside the uterus, and still "coding" for endometrial cells, then this might cause endometrial lesions.[9]

The **embryonic origin theory** suggest that the condition develops during fetal development. According to this theory the female reproductive organs develop abnormally in utero due to the body not properly differentiating between components.[9]

As discussed previously **hormones**, such as prostaglandins, likely play a large role in endometriosis. Their exact role is still a subject of much debate among endocrinologists. Much more research needs to be done on the effects of estrogen and progesterone on endometriosis.[9]

Many researchers also believe that the **immune system,** specifically the **lymphatic system,** contributes to the spread of endometriosis. The lymphatic system is a component of the circulatory system, which is responsible for taking critical fluids to, and removing fluids from, different tissues in the body. Usually, lymphatic fluids carry a variety of things necessary for the body and its immune function, such as red blood cells, white blood cells, and plasma. It is proposed that in women with endometriosis, it might also be carrying endometrial cells to other parts of the body where they should not be. This would explain why endometriosis has been found in almost every major organ outside the uterus. It also provides a connection between immune system health and endometriosis. [9]

Conversation about **"free radicals"** has increased in recent years. They are blamed for everything from inflammation, to weight gain, to skin aging. Many products claim to "eliminate or reduce free radical damage." But what are they? Free radicals are highly unstable molecules of oxygen that form when atoms or molecules gain or lose electrons. In excess they can harm your body. In a young, healthy body the body deals with free radicals via antioxidants. However, with age or illness oxidative stress can occur, which is the imbalance between the production of free radicals and the ability of the body to neutralize them. It is suspected that oxidative stress might play a role in endometriosis.[9]

Cell **apoptosis** is another avenue that is currently being explored in relation to endometriosis. Apoptosis is the programmed death of cells. It is usually a highly controlled mechanism that is essential to the prevention of disease in the body. An example would be the presence of cancer, which occurs when apoptosis fails, and the body is not able to destroy malignant cells. It has been discovered that similarly to cancer, endometriosis cells are also able to avoid apoptosis. [9]

Most modern scientists do agree that there is at least some **genetic component** to endometriosis. If a woman has a close female family member with endometriosis, such as a mother, daughter, sister, or aunt, they are more likely to themselves have endometriosis. They are also more likely to have severe symptoms if their family members have severe symptoms. While it is clear the condition can be inherited, scientists are still investigating what genes are associated with endometriosis.[9]

Environmental toxins have also been proposed to contribute to endometriosis and severity of symptoms. Modern humans are exposed to environmental toxins almost daily, chemical pollutants can affect the body and immune system, and potentially lead to development of endometriosis.[10]

Diagnosis:

The first step to diagnosis of endometriosis is in the identification of signs and symptoms. How these present though can vary significantly. Many women notice something is amiss as soon as they begin their first menstrual cycle. They might realize their severe pain and heavy bleeding is different than many of their friend's experiences. On the other hand, some women never have chronic pain, and it is not until the try to conceive that they realize something is wrong.

Unfortunately, it can be very hard for women to get a diagnosis of endometriosis, due to the lack of training on women's health issues that many general doctors have. Sometimes symptoms are dismissed completely, as an "overreaction" to the normal discomfort of menstruation. In some ways many current medical professionals haven't come far from the dismissive attitudes of the "hysteria" era. If a woman does get taken seriously, the doctor will take a symptom report and conduct a pelvic exam. If most of the symptoms are consistent with endometriosis, and especially if the pelvic exam detects any nodules or abnormalities, then it is common for the woman to be referred to a gynecologist who often prescribes some sort of birth control. This is usually either hormonal pills or an IUD. While in some cases birth control can mitigate symptoms, it is not a cure, and in some women can exacerbate the problem.

It is common for further diagnostics to be delayed until after the woman tries birth control. If that doesn't work, then the woman might be referred get an ultrasound, CT, or MRI to see if there are other issues such as fibroids or ovarian cysts. Blood tests will also be run to make sure there are no other conditions present. While in many cases an unofficial diagnosis of endometriosis will be granted based on symptoms and elimination of other diseases, there is not currently a non-invasive way to definitively diagnosis endometriosis. The standard diagnostic tool is a laparoscopy.

A laparoscopy is a surgical procedure in which a small incision in the abdominal wall is made and a fiber-optic instrument with a camera is inserted so that the surgeon can view the internal organs. While a laparoscopy is generally an outpatient procedure, meaning that you do not have to spend the night in the hospital, it is still a surgery and requires anesthesia. Just as with any other surgical procedure, there can be discomfort, infection, damage, and scarring.

The most important thing to remember when facing a potential endometriosis diagnosis is to always be your own advocate. Monitor your symptoms carefully, keep track of menstrual cycles. Write down everything. Insist on a referral to a gynecologist or another specialist familiar with endometriosis. Seek multiple opinions. Ask for clarification. Join support groups and talk to other women affected by endometriosis. If you have reason to not want to go on hormonal birth control, or if you feel a treatment is not working, tell your doctor. When it comes down to it, you know your body best. You are the patient, and you have the right to guide your own treatment.

"Traditional Treatment"

Throughout history, many treatments, varying from mildly successful in pain management to terrifying and ineffective were prescribed.[8] While it is thankfully no longer common to use leeches, or shake women upside down in the hope that the uterus will "fall back into place," many modern techniques have side effects or are uncomfortable and invasive for women suffering with endometriosis.

Different methods of controlling the pain, since there is no official cure for endometriosis, are commonly prescribed. This includes everything from over-the-counter **anti-inflammatory pain killers** such as NSAIDS (i.e. ibuprofen) to **opioids** (i.e. codeine) in severe cases. Some doctors might also prescribe transdermal **pain killer patches**, if other methods of pain control have not been effective.

Other forms of pain control include muscle relaxation, either in the form of **chemical muscle relaxers** (i.e., cyclobenzaprine), **heat therapy** (heating pad or hot water bottle), or a transcutaneous electrical nerve stimulation (**TENS**) unit. Physical therapy, muscle injections, and acupuncture are all other forms of treatment for the muscles.

Hormonal treatment has become very common in dealing with endometriosis, even though it is <u>not</u> a cure, but only treats the symptoms just as other medicines do. The logic behind hormonal treatment is to prevent menstruation and therefore prevent endometrial cells from shedding and causing inflammation and pain. **Hormonal birth control** can come in the form of birth control pills, a vaginal ring, a patch, an implant, or an IUD.

While birth control is being prescribed as a sort of "cure-all" for many women's health issues these days, it is not without its side effects, sometimes serious ones. Some women find these side effects almost as bad as the endometriosis itself. The side effects include, but are not limited to, physical effects such as blood clots, cardiovascular problems and heart attacks, acne, weight gain, nausea and vomiting, bloating, migraines, and emotional effects such as severe depression and mood swings. In some cases, the side effects can be irreversible, and some women may sustain permanent damage to their reproductive system after getting off birth control.

Unfortunately, many women are pressured into "just trying" hormonal birth control when it might not be the best option for them. If one doesn't work or has horrible side effects, they might be encouraged to just try a different type, going through rounds and rounds of different drugs and just throwing their body off even more.

Surgery is another common modern treatment, and by far the most drastic and permanent of the ones mentioned. Total hysterectomies are the second most common surgery among women in the United States. [11] A hysterectomy is a surgery to remove a woman's uterus, during which the fallopian tubes and ovaries might also be removed. A hysterectomy is especially common if a woman with endometriosis is of a certain advanced age or has already had children. Many doctors view the uterus as no longer necessary if the woman isn't likely to have any more children, completely disregarding the fact that is a major organ, and its loss is not without side effects.

A hysterectomy results in early menopause, and can cause damage to the vagina, urinary incontinence, hot flashes, bone weakening, heart disease, and weight gain. It can also reduce the ability for a woman to experience sexual pleasure. Of course, there is also the obvious of not being able to have children after the procedure. If a woman has not yet had a child, or was planning on having more children, this can be emotionally devastating.

Small errors during surgery can also result in the cutting of nerve endings or ligaments. Many women suffer from severe bowel problems following hysterectomy. Vaginal prolapse, in which the vagina slips out of position can also occur. If ovaries are left in during the procedure it is common for a second surgery to be performed within several years to remove them.

Despite how drastic a hysterectomy is it is also <u>not</u> a cure for endometriosis. Any endometrial cells or lesions in the abdominal cavity outside the uterus will still be there after the surgery. The leftover endometrial tissue can still spread, shed, and bleed just as before.

The uterus is also a large, important organ in women. Its removal is not without consequences. The body notices its absence. The uterus is directly in between the bladder and intestines. When it is removed those inevitably shift, which can lead to problems.

Hysterectomies are becoming increasingly pushed by the western medical industry as a "solution" to endometriosis, but they are not and should not be considered the best option. When facing pressure from doctors it can be hard to say no to a surgery, especially when they insist it is necessary. Always remember though, you are the patient, it is your life, and your body. You always have the right to say no!

When looking at the options put forward by modern western medicine it can be easy to feel discouraged. Oftentimes women are never told that they have any option other than a life of painkillers, hormones, and surgery. They might not be fully informed about their own condition, and when scared and in pain it is easy to make decisions you might regret later. Unfortunately, many times women with endometriosis are pressured into drastic treatments. It is important to remember that what are often presented as "the only options" might not in fact be the only options. For those willing to do some of their own research, there are non-traditional, "natural" ways to begin healing a body suffering from endometriosis.

Part Two: Endometriosis and Holistic Medicine

Steps to Holistic Healing:

What is holistic healing? And is there really "another-way" to deal with endometriosis outside of the modern medical machine? Yes!

Knowing that there is no official cure for endometriosis can feel crippling, but it does not have to. There is hope. When you start to treat your body in its entirety better, you might be amazed by how your endometriosis, and all the symptoms associated with endometriosis, begin to improve. Holistic healing is just that, a type of healing that looks at the whole person, the body, mind, and spirit. It combines conventional modern treatment and alternative therapies, to promote optimal health, and thereby treat disease. Holistic healing is often practiced in conjunction with homeopathy, a medical system based on a natural approach to treatment, in which natural substances are used to encourage the body's own healing process.

When you are beginning your journey to holistic healing there are several main principles to keep in mind:

1. **Be proactive.**

Take control of your own health. Educate yourself, do your own research and talk to a variety of different healthcare experts. Listen. Ask questions. Stand up for yourself when interacting with healthcare professionals. Make sure you understand why you are doing things when it comes to your health.

2. **Find healthcare professionals and therapeutic treatments that are compatible with you.**

Make sure you find a holistic healthcare practitioner that listens to you and has your best interests at heart. Make sure they are guiding you to the best course of action, and not just telling you what you want to hear. If something is not working, speak up. If something is working, keep doing it!

3. **Be patient with yourself.**

Take care of yourself. Be gentle with your mind and body. Realize that health is a journey, and progress will not always happen overnight.

4. **Be open to lifestyle changes.**

The best option for your health is not always the easy one. Sometimes we must recognize that our previous behaviors and ways of living just are not working. It can be hard to make radical changes, but sometimes they are necessary for us to live our best lives.

Diet and Endometriosis

Almost everyone is familiar with the saying "you are what you eat." There is a good reason for that — it is true. The food you consume today will impact your health tomorrow and in the future. Your body is constantly regenerating itself. Old cells die, and new cells are produced. Food is the fuel for that production of new cells. Good food results in healthy cells, and bad food results in not-so-healthy cells. In order to have the best functioning body you can have; you want to consume the best fuel you can.

A lot of times when we start talking about healthy eating the dreaded "d-word" comes to mind: diet. But what is a diet? And what is the difference between "going on a diet" and changing your diet?

The term "going on a diet" might make you think of temporary fad dieting designed to help someone lose weight quickly. It might also make you think of the kind of planned diet programs promoted by celebrities, or more dangerously, restrictive, and disordered eating. Changing your diet is not the same as "going on a diet." It is not a temporary change with a set goal like losing a certain amount of weight or gaining a specific amount of muscle. Changing your diet means you are permanently improving the way you eat so that you optimize your health for the rest of your life.

The average western diet is, simply put — horrendous. It is associated with higher levels of obesity, heart disease, diabetes, Crohn's disease, cancer, and poor metabolic health.[12] The average modern western diet is full of excess sodium, saturated fat, refined grains, and added sugars. Most protein comes from animal products, specifically red and processed meats.

Fast food chains are everywhere, serving up greasy, high calorie foods with little nutritional value. The grocery store has entire aisles dedicated to "junk foods," which are often less expensive than fresh, healthy food. Many snacks are intentionally designed to be borderline addictive, so you will keep buying more. Pre-prepared, packaged, and heavily processed meals are easy to grab off the shelf. They are full of preservatives and other harmful additives, but in today's fast paced world that can be easy to overlook for the sake of convenience.

So how does a health-conscious person today navigate the world of not-so-healthy food? To beat your endometriosis symptoms, do you have to resign yourself to a lifetime of eating nothing but raw carrots? Of course not! With some simple tips and practice you can develop healthy eating habits. You can also gain the ability to distinguish food that is good for your body from junk food masquerading as healthy food with just a glance. You do not have to eat less, or completely give up all the foods you love. You just have to eat consciously, and intentionally, with the goal of meeting all of your body's nutritional needs.

The Importance of a "Balanced Diet"

What is a balanced diet? And what can make it hard to achieve? A balanced diet is one that meets all of a person's nutritional needs, while also staying under their recommended calorie intake. The average recommended calorie intake for an adult woman is somewhere between 1,600–2,400 calories, depending on how physically active they are. It might not seem hard to get all the nutrient you need within that range, but it can be if you are making the wrong choices.

So much processed food today is made up of what are called "empty calories." Things like cookies, donuts, pizza, soda, and ice cream will all provide your body with calories. They are all technically "fuel" — but not good fuel. If you eat too many "empty calorie" foods, you will not have room for other foods which provide essential nutrients to your body. When your body is nutritionally deficient it is also more likely that you will experience cravings. Thus, begins the vicious cycle of eating more and more unhealthy foods and feeling worse and worse.

To make sure you are getting all the nutrients you need there are five basic food groups you should eat <u>every day</u>:

1. **Vegetables** - Most of your diet should be made up of vegetables. You should aim to consume at least 4-5 servings per day. A good tip when choosing vegetables is the more color, the better! Vegetables of different types contain a wide variety of vitamins, which have been shown to be lower in endometriosis patients. The five main kinds of vegetables are leafy greens, red and orange vegetables, starchy vegetables, legumes (beans and peas) and other vegetables, such as eggplant or squash. You should aim to eat at least one type of vegetable in each category every week. Not only will this ensure you are getting more vitamins, doing so will also prevent you from getting bored with eating the same thing. You can serve vegetables by having a salad with your meal. You can also have them as a side dish with each meal, by roasting, stir frying, or boiling them with seasoning. Incorporating them into one pot meals like soups, stews, and pasta dishes is another option.

2. **Fruit** - a balanced diet also includes plenty of whole, fresh fruit. While juice can be tasty on occasion, you want to try to eat whole fruit whenever possible, as it contains more nutrients. You should aim to eat at least 1-2 servings per day. Having a side of fruit for breakfast can be a great way to kickstart your day with natural sugar and vitamins. Berries, peaches, nectarines, citrus fruits, red grapes, plums, pomegranates, apples, and pears are several options that are high in nutrients. Citrus fruits particularly, such as oranges or grapefruit, have been associated with reduced endometriosis symptoms.[15]

3. **Grain** - you might be surprised that grains are considered part of a healthy diet. It seems they have somewhat of a bad stigma these days. Refined white flour is one of the most common grain products these days, which has limited nutritional value. Heavily processed grains can cause inflammation and gut problems in many people. Natural, whole grains though can do quite the opposite. Whole grains are rich in vitamins, minerals, fiber, and good-for-you carbohydrates that provide your body with an essential source of energy. You should aim to have 3-5 servings of grain per day. Whole wheat breads and pasta are

better options that those made with white flour. If you want to avoid processing all together whole buckwheat, barley, and rye are good options. For those that do not eat gluten brown rice, basmati rice, wild rice, quinoa, amaranth, sorghum, and steel-cut oats are all gluten-free grains.

4. **Protein** - protein is essential for wound healing and bone and muscle maintenance. Protein also allows our body to make enzymes, hormones, and other chemicals necessary for functioning. You can get protein from both animal and plant sources. Seafood, lean meat, poultry, and eggs are all good options for women suffering with endometriosis. Fish especially is good because it is high in Omega-3s, which are anti-inflammatory. Women with endometriosis should mostly avoid red meat, or only eat it in small quantities (1-2 servings per week). Studies have shown that women who consumed more than two servings of red meat per day had a 56% higher risk of endometriosis than those that did not. [16] Healthy plant sources of protein include lentils, beans, peas, and nuts. Soy products also provide protein but should be avoided or eaten sparingly because they contain estrogen which can aggravate endometriosis symptoms. If you are

vegan or vegetarian and rely on soy products for a good portion of your protein needs, it is better to choose organic tofu or tempeh over processed meat substitutes.

5. **Dairy and Vitamin D -** dairy products should be eaten sparingly and chosen careful. They can cause inflammation and those that contain growth hormones or antibiotics might also worsen endometriosis symptoms. However, dairy products are also excellent sources of Vitamin D which keeps keep bones, teeth, and muscles healthy. A Vitamin D deficiency can lead to all sort of problems including osteoporosis and problems with the immune, brain, and nervous systems. Vitamin D has also been shown to reduce pro-inflammatory cytokines that contribute to endometriosis inflammation.[14] When choosing dairy select organic, low-fat versions. Hard cheeses, such as Swiss or Parmesan, as well as cottage cheese, are also lower in lactose for those that are lactose intolerant.

Goat, sheep milk, and cheese can also be good options for women with endometriosis. They still contain Vitamin D but have A2 Casein instead of the dairy A1

Casein in cow's milk which has been found to cause higher levels of inflammation.

For those that would prefer to eliminate dairy entirely; cod liver oil, trout, salmon, mushrooms, eggs, and broccoli are all good sources of Vitamin D. Regular exposure to sunlight is also a good non-dietary way to get Vitamin D while also boosting mood levels. You do not want too much direct sunlight, as that can lead to skin cancer, so aim for about 10–30 mins per day.

Key Nutrients for Endometriosis

B vitamins - B-vitamins are essential to a well-functioning liver, which degrades estradiol to estriol. Estriol helps circulating estrogen be bound to fiber and excreted. B-vitamins are found in high levels in green, leafy vegetables, which also contain **Magnesium.** Magnesium helps to relax muscles, including those found in the intestines and uterus, which can result in less severe cramping. The best vegetables from which to get both B-vitamins and magnesium are greens such as cabbage, Brussels sprouts, broccoli, cauliflower, spinach, kale, turnips, collards, and radish greens. Nutritional yeast is an excellent source of B-12. It has a slightly cheesy flavor and can be used in soups, salad dressings, in place of parmesan, or wherever else you might desire a cheesy flavor.

Omega fatty acids - Omega fatty acids are good sources of fat that are anti-inflammatory. They are found in oily fish, such as mackerel, tuna, herring, and sardines. They are also found in nuts and seeds such as flaxseed, chia seeds, and walnuts, and oils such as extra virgin olive oil.

Iron-rich foods - any women who have endometriosis are also iron-deficient due to heavy blood loss during their menstrual periods. Iron can be found in both plant and animal source. Plant sources include green, leafy vegetables, beets, apricots, and chocolate. Red meat is animal source that is high in iron, but it can also be acquired from eggs and fish, which tend to cause less endometriosis symptoms.

Vitamin C - Vitamin C is well known as being beneficial for the immune system. It is also excellent for wound healing. Citrus fruits and bell peppers are a great source of Vitamin C.

Vitamin A - Eat your carrots! (and pumpkins, and sweet potatoes, and butternut squash). During World War II propaganda campaigns urged soldiers to eat their carrots for better vision because Vitamin A is crucial for healthy eyes. Beyond just good vision, Vitamin A has also been shown to help women who have heavy bleeding during their menstrual periods. [19]

Vitamin E - Vitamin E functions as an antioxidant. Studies in women with endometriosis, showed that increased Vitamin E level resulted in significant pain decrease in 43% of women. [18]

Good sources of Vitamin E include leafy greens, pumpkin, red bell peppers, sunflower seeds, almonds, and peanuts. Vitamin E supplements can also be very helpful for women with endometriosis.

Fiber - Fiber is essential for the diet of woman with endometriosis because it keeps your intestinal tract healthy and aids in the excretion of excess estrogens. Good sources of daily fiber are found in fruit, vegetables, nuts, seeds, legumes, and whole grains.

Water - While not technically a "nutrient", water is an essential part of your diet. You should make sure you drink four to six 8-ounce glasses of water a day. Without water the body cannot function properly. Water also removes metabolic waste products.

Anti-Inflammatory Foods for Endometriosis

A fundamental feature of endometriosis is chronic inflammation.[1] Therefore, the optimal endometriosis diet is one that includes highly anti-inflammatory foods. Some foods that are especially good at fighting inflammation are listed below:

Berries

Avocadoes

Cherries

Bell Peppers

Broccoli

Green tea

Turmeric

Bananas

Pineapple

Ginger

Bone broth

Salmon

Spirulina

Fermented foods such as sauerkraut or kimchi

Eggs

Nuts and nut butters

Organic vs. Non-Organic:

What is "Organic" food? It is probably a term you have heard before, but you might not know exact what it means, or why it really matters. Organic foods are grown and processed differently than non-organic foods. To receive an organic label, the food has to meet certain criteria from the government.

Just because a label says something is "natural," "pesticide-free," or "hormone-free" does not mean it is also organic. To get an organic seal from the USDA the food must be at least 95% organic. Organic food is produced without the use of conventional pesticides, bioengineering, synthetic fertilizer, sewage sludge, or radiation.

Research has shown that some pesticides have been associated with decreased antioxidant capacity in fruits and vegetables. Some have also been shown to negatively affect hormonal pathways. As talked about previously, antioxidants help prevent free-radical damage which is thought to contribute to endometriosis symptoms. Hormones also play a role in endometriosis and disrupting the body's hormone balances could negatively affect symptoms.

While organic food is generally better for you than non-organic food, it can also be more expensive. So, do you have to buy everything organic? While it would be great if everyone could just buy fresh organic food directly from their next-door farmer, that's not always an option. What can you afford to save money on and not buy organic? Scientists have come up with two lists, encompassing commonly eaten fruits and vegetables that you might buy at your local supermarket: the "Dirty Dozen" and the "Clean Fifteen". The "Dirty Dozen" is the list of foods that typically have the most pesticides when not organic. The "Clean Fifteen" generally have the least amount of pesticides and are okay to buy non-organic.

The Dirty Dozen:

1. Strawberries.
2. Apples.
3. Nectarines.
4. Peaches.
5. Celery.
6. Grapes.
7. Cherries.
8. Spinach.
9. Tomatoes.
10. Cherry Tomatoes.
11. Cucumbers.
12. Bell Peppers

9. Papayas.
10. Kiwi.
11. Eggplant.
12. Honeydew.
13. Grapefruit.
14. Cantaloupe.
15. Cauliflower.

Clean Fifteen:

1. Avocados.
2. Corn.
3. Pineapple.
4. Cabbage.
5. Sweet Peas.
6. Onions.
7. Asparagus.
8. Mangoes.

Gluten and Endometriosis:

Gluten is a protein found in grains and wheat products which can cause diarrhea, abdominal pain, and bloating in people with gluten sensitivity. It can also result malabsorption of some vitamins and minerals that regulate hormones, as well as causing cause inflammation and sometimes autoimmune reactions.[14] Some women with endometriosis are not bothered at all by gluten, while others find their symptoms significantly improve when they cut out gluten from their diets.

A good way to determine if gluten is making your endometriosis worse is to do an elimination diet. There are two steps to an elimination diet. First over the course of two weeks you will remove all products containing gluten from your diet completely. No cheating or the process will not work! *You must keep careful track of all your symptoms during this step*. For the second step you slowly start re-introducing healthy sources of gluten like whole wheat into your diet over a course of four weeks. *Once again keep careful track of your symptoms.* Compare the symptoms from the two steps with your doctor or other healthcare professional. If you have a significant increase of symptoms during the second, re-introduction period you might be better served adopting a healthy, permanently gluten-free diet. Gluten-free pasta and breads, whole grain rice, quinoa, sorghum, amaranth, and whole oats can all help to take the place in your diet of grains containing gluten.

Foods to always avoid:

1. **Artificial sugar** - sugar from fruit is fine, but artificial sugar leads to inflammation. If you are craving something sweet try fruit or dark chocolate, which is high in antioxidants.
2. **Caffeine** - giving up coffee completely might seem like a nightmare, but you really should limit your caffeine intake. Too much creates inflammation, increases cramps, irritates the digestive system, and can even cause ulcers. If you need caffeine to be a fully functional human being try to limit it to less than 200 mg a day- about the size of a regular cup of coffee. Green tea, especially matcha, is also a good option if you are trying to wean off coffee. It still has some caffeine, but it is also anti-inflammatory.
3. **Deep fried foods** - contain unhealthy trans fats which increase inflammation in the body and can cause digestive problems. Options such as homemade baked French fries are a great alternative to the deep-fried version.

4. **Processed red meat** - including hot dogs, hamburgers, ham, bacon, and sausage is once again inflammatory, as well as being tied to higher risk of heart disease.
5. **Heavily processed "junk" foods** - skip the twinkies and Cheetos. Lots of junk food is intentionally engineered to have something called "vanishing caloric density." Essentially, it's nutritional deficiency, high calorie food that tricks your brain into thinking it has no calories. As you eat it gives your mind pleasure, while also making you feel like you have not eaten anything. It is intentionally designed to make you crave more!
6. **Alcohol** - alcohol is technically toxic to the body, it puts a lot of stress on the liver in addition to turning into sugar once inside the body. It also raises estrogen levels. Try not to drink regularly, if at all, and if you decide to partake, choose something with a lower alcohol content. Skip the vodka shots and go for one glass of red wine, which has antioxidant and anti-inflammatory properties.

How to identify sneaky unhealthy food:

There are a lot of fake healthy foods out there that are marketed as if they are good for you but are really junk food in disguise. So how do you tell the difference? Realistically you probably will buy some amount of processed food, even though you want to minimize it. Sometimes life happens and you just do not have time to cook all of your meals from scratch. But how do you make sure you are choosing the healthiest option? Here are some terms to know (and avoid) when reading labels:

High-Fructose Corn Syrup - corn syrups are a common and cheap replacement for real sugar which are is associated with inflammation as well as potential cell damage.

Palm Oil - palm oil is high in saturated fat, as well as its production being bad for the environment.

Artificial Colors - certain artificial colors, such as Blue 1, Blue 2, Red 3, Green 3, and Yellow 6, have been banned in some European countries because of their negative health effects.

"Fat Free" - not all foods that are marketed as fat free are bad, but make sure to read the ingredients. Often the removed fat must be replaced with something else, usually extra sugar and salt. You also want to make sure you are consuming healthy fats, as they are essential to a good diet.

Partially Hydrogenated Oil - just another term for harmful trans fats.

Hidden sugars - Anhydrous dextrose, dextrose, corn syrup, fructose, high-fructose corn syrup, honey, invert sugar, malt syrup, maltose, maple syrup, molasses, nectars, and sucrose are all terms that indicate sugar content.

Here are some common culprits (foods that seem healthy but are not), and what to eat instead:

1. Dried Fruit- tons of added sugar! → **Instead eat fresh fruit or dry your own.**
2. Vegetable chips- high in sodium and fat and low in nutrients. → **Instead eat: fresh sliced veggies and hummus.**
3. Salad dressing- many store-bought salad dressings are high in sodium, carbs, and sugar. → **Instead make your own salad dressing with healthy oils and seasonings.**
4. Sports drinks- high in sugar, sodium, carbs, and artificial dye. → **Instead have coconut water, which is all natural and high in potassium.**
5. Flavored Yogurt- artificial sweeteners and dyes → **Instead eat plain, organic, low-fat Greek yogurt with fresh fruit.**

6. Diet soft drinks- no soda is healthy, but diet soft drinks can be especially bad, and deceiving. They contain many terrible artificial sweeteners like sucralose, saccharin, and aspartame. → **Instead try sparkling water or kombucha.**
7. Instant oatmeal- low in fiber and protein and high in added sugar. → **Instead try steel cut oats with fresh fruit.**
8. Reduced-fat peanut butter- the same amount of calories as regular peanut butter, but with more sugar. **→Regular, preferably organic peanut butter, with no added sugar.**

The key thing to remember whenever you begin to make dietary changes it to do what works best for you. Not every woman with endometriosis will respond in the same way to the same foods. You know your body the best — listen to it!

Keep a food journal <u>and</u> a symptom journal. Keep track of correlations between certain foods and more severe symptoms. If you notice that certain foods trigger your symptoms, avoid them. Also make note of foods that seem to improve symptoms. If something makes you feel good try incorporating that into more meals!

Example Meal Plan for Endometriosis:

Breakfast Ideas:

- Whole grain oats with fresh blueberries, crushed walnuts, and almond milk.
- Scrambled eggs or omelets with onions, mushrooms, spinach, and bell peppers and whole wheat toast or corn tortillas on the side.
- Coconut milk, banana, and frozen berry smoothie.
- Homemade gluten free pancakes or waffles with fresh fruit.
- Whole wheat or gluten free toast with peanut butter, sliced bananas, and flax seeds.
- Green smoothie with spirulina, banana, almond milk, spinach, and avocado.
- Eggs fried in 1 tsp olive oil with homemade hash browns.

Lunch Ideas:

- Spinach salad with chicken, avocado, cucumber, tomato, goat cheese, and oil and vinegar dressing.
- Lunch bowl with roasted sweet potatoes, quinoa, black beans, and avocado.

- Homemade tuna or egg-salad on whole wheat or gluten-free bread with lettuce and tomatoes.
- Whole wheat or gluten-free panini with sliced turkey, spinach, sundried tomatoes, pesto, and cheese.
- Rice noodle "ramen" with carrots, spinach, mushrooms, broccoli, and a hardboiled egg.
- Shrimp lettuce wraps with homemade peanut sauce.

Dinner Ideas:

- One pan salmon and broccoli with wild rice.
- Kale and white bean stew with tomatoes and Italian seasoning.
- Bell peppers stuffed with wild rice and chicken, served with tomato sauce.
- Grilled portobello mushroom with quinoa and stir-fried zucchini.
- Chicken stir-fry with rice noodles, broccoli, mushrooms, bell peppers, and cabbage.
- Lentil or chickpea curry.
- Roasted butternut squash stuffed with quinoa and kale.
- Zucchini noodles with tomato sauce and turkey meatballs.

- Roasted beets, carrots, and tomatoes with turkey, wild rice, and cranberry sauce.

Snack Ideas:

- Homemade trail mix.
- Popcorn with nutritional yeast.
- A handful of walnuts, almonds, or cashews.
- Dark chocolate.
- Sliced apples and peanut butter.
- Carrots and hummus.

Deficiencies and supplements:

It's a paradox of modern society, in many ways the average person in the western world is consuming too much food. So, we should be getting plenty of nutrients, right? Unfortunately, that is not the case. Many people around the globe suffer from micronutrient deficiencies which can lead to serious health problems. This can happen due to eating high calorie, nutrient lacking food, which is all too common. Heavily processed foods are common culprits, tending to be incredibly low in nutritional value.

Even with eating a relatively balanced diet it can sometimes be difficult to get all the nutrients you need. Many times, in the modern Western world, our produce is not actually fresh. It is picked early and shipped, not to ripen until it is in the supermarket, resulting in less nutrients than freshly picked fruits and veggies. Genetic modification of food has also led to less nutritional value.

Vitamins and mineral supplements can help to make sure you are getting all the nutrients you need. There are also some additional supplements that are not as common and you might not acquire dietarily, that could help with your endometriosis symptoms. Keep track of all supplements, and make sure you are not exceeding the daily recommended dose on anything. It is always a good idea to consult with your health care professional before adding any new supplements to your diet.

Probiotics - probiotics are essential to a healthy gut and digestive systems and can help mitigate GI distressed caused by endometriosis. They can be found in yogurt and fermented foods, but some people choose to take them via daily probiotic supplements.

Omega 3 fatty acids - as mentioned earlier, Omega 3 fatty acids are excellent for reducing inflammation. You can find flax and fish oil either in liquid or capsule form that is high in concentrated Omega 3.

Magnesium - many women with endometriosis are also magnesium deficient due to estrogen dominance in their bodies. Chocolate is high in magnesium which is why chocolate cravings are often associated with the menstrual cycle. Magnesium supplements can be a good way of maintaining adequate magnesium levels.

Calcium - calcium deficiency can cause muscle aches and cramps and pelvic pain. Calcium levels are also generally lower in women during the premenstrual period. Calcium supplements might help to reduce premenstrual syndrome and cramping.

Vitamin C, Vitamin A, and Vitamin E - these vitamins are all essential and can be found in separate supplements or most basic daily multivitamins.

Zinc - deficiency in zinc has been associated with increased inflammation. Zinc supplements might help to ease symptoms.

Selenium - another mineral with anti-inflammatory properties is selenium. It is found naturally in brazil nuts but can also be taken as a supplement. Selenium deficiency can result in muscle weakness and fatigue.

Another good way to ensure you are getting sufficient nutrients is to make **smoothies or protein shakes.** Frequently, endometriosis pain can lead to a lack of appetite. It's difficult to eat when your abdominal area is in severe pain!

Drinking a meal or two can be a lot easier. Obviously, you don't want to replace all of your solid food meals with blended ones but having a least a few protein shakes a week is a good idea.

Getting enough protein is especially important for women with endometriosis because protein is necessary for the body's healing processes. Even the etymology of the word "protein" indicates just how necessary of a nutrient it is— it comes from the Greek word protos, which means "first" or "primary." Protein is necessarily to build and repair your muscle, skin, and all your body's other tissues. You also need protein to help fight infections, balancing your bodily fluids, and oxygenate your body.

Protein shakes are great for insuring you are getting enough protein, and you can also include other essential nutrients in the shake! First, you want to begin by selecting the protein base, generally a protein powder. When choosing a protein powder, it is a good idea to avoid soy, wheat, or a dairy based protein powders as they can lead to endometriosis flare ups. Rice or pea powder proteins, preferably organic, are the best choice. Adding nuts, nut butters, or seeds is a great way to get extra protein, as well as healthy fats. Next, add some fresh fruits or veggies to get vitamins and minerals. Some great shake ingredients are listed below:

Dark leafy greens - greens like spinach and kale are great to add to almost any smoothie! If you are using your shake as a meal replacement you want to make sure you have more than just fruit, include some veggies as well! Otherwise, it will not be a balanced meal.

Leafy greens help you get important nutrients like fiber and folate, as well as other phytonutrients like carotenoids, saponins, and flavonoids. Kale specifically is considered a cruciferous vegetable, and contains glucosinolates, which are a type of anti-inflammatory phytonutrient.

Ground flaxseed - flaxseed is a great source of extra protein and fiber, as well as Omega-3 fatty acids. Flaxseed can also help with bowel regularity and help relieve constipation.

Hemp hearts - hemp hearts are the soft inner part of hemp seeds, which come from the cannabis plant, but do not contain THC which is the psychoactive compound of the plant. Hemp seeds have a mild, nutty flavor and are very nutritious. They are a great source of protein and Omega-6 and Omega-3 fatty acids.

Peanut butter or Almond butter - nut butters can give your shake some extra bulk and flavor, as well as flavor. They are also great sources of healthy fat. Just make sure to choose nut butters that are organic and do not contain any extra additives.

Berries - some type of fruit is a must for any smoothie or shake! Berries are especially good. They are full of antioxidants, vitamins, and fiber. They also add a sweet taste to your smoothie or shake. If you would like you can use frozen berries as a replacement for ice. Frozen fruit is just as nutritious as fresh, as all the nutrients are preserved in the freezing process. As always though, make sure to purchase organic frozen berries.

Spirulina powder - spirulina is a type of aquatic cyanobacteria, or blue-green algae that lives in the water. Spirulina was a superfood consumed by the ancient Aztecs of Mexico. It is so nutritionally dense that it has even been proposed to be grown in space and used as food for astronauts.

A single tablespoon of dried spirulina powder contains:

- 4 grams of protein.
- 11% of the recommended daily amount of Vitamin B1, also known as thiamine.
- 15% of the recommended daily amount of Vitamin B2, also known as riboflavin.
- 4% of the recommended daily amount of Vitamin B3, also known as niacin.
- 21% of the recommended daily amount of copper.

- 11% of the recommended daily amount of Iron.

It also contains amounts of magnesium, potassium, and manganese, and both Omega-6 and Omega-3 fatty acids.

Spirulina has also been shown to lower bad (low-density lipoprotein) cholesterol and triglyceride levels, raise good (high-density lipoprotein) cholesterol, have anti-cancer properties, reduce blood pressure, reduce allergies, fight anemia, improve muscle strength, and help with blood sugar control.

While spirulina is generally safe, and great for you, you want to make sure you are purchasing it from a good source. Improperly produced spirulina can be contaminated with toxic metals, harmful bacteria, and microcystins, which are toxins that can be produced from certain algae.

You also should avoid spirulina if you have an autoimmune condition such as multiple sclerosis, lupus, or rheumatoid arthritis. Spirulina enhances the immune system quite a bit, and thus can make conditions that are a result of an overactive immune system worse. It can also interfere with immunosuppressant drugs that are prescribed for such conditions. Spirulina should also be avoided if you take blood thinning medications, as well as during pregnancy, because it can increase risk of bleeding.

Mango - mango is a very tasty fruit to add to smoothies. It is also very high in Vitamin C and Vitamin A as well as containing Vitamin E, Vitamin K, Vitamin B6, Vitamin B9, potassium, and copper.

Turmeric - as covered previous, turmeric is amazing for inflammation, and can be a great addition to a smoothie or shake.

Pineapple - pineapple is a great way to add some natural sweetness to your smoothie or shake. It contains the enzyme bromelain, which aids in the digestion of protein and is also anti-inflammatory. Pineapple also has tons of Vitamin C.

Raw cacao powder - what is not to like about adding chocolate to your meal! Raw cacao is a good source of magnesium, iron, calcium, potassium, and phosphorous. It is also a natural mood enhancer.

Bananas - the yellow fruit is full of the nutrients potassium and manganese, which help prevent muscle cramps, heal wounds, and increase bone strength.

Cherries - cherries contain anthocyanins, a compound that has been linked with fighting inflammation, as well as Vitamin C.

Protein shake ideas:

Banana and Chocolate Shake:

- 1 scoop protein powder
- 1 frozen banana
- 2 tablespoons raw cacao powder
- 2 tablespoons almond butter
- 1 cup almond milk
- 1/2 teaspoon cinnamon
- 1 cup of ice

Cherry-Lime Shake:

- 1 scoop protein powder
- 1 cup cherries
- 1 avocado
- 1 cup spinach.
- 1 cup almond milk
- 3 tablespoons fresh lime juice
- 1 cup of ice

"Golden Milk" Turmeric Shake:

- 1 scoop protein powder
- 1 cup frozen mango
- 1 frozen banana

- 1 cup pineapple
- Coconut milk
- 1 teaspoon turmeric
- 1/2 teaspoon ginger

Green Mango Shake:

- 1 scoop protein powder
- 1 cup frozen mango
- 1 frozen banana
- 1 cup almond milk
- 1 cup fresh spinach
- 2 tablespoons hemp hearts

Super Spirulina Shake:

- 1 scoop protein powder
- 1 frozen banana
- 1 cup coconut milk
- 1 cup spinach
- 1 teaspoon spirulina
- 1 tablespoon flax seeds

Strawberry-Almond butter Shake:

- 1 scoop protein powder
- 1 frozen banana

- 2 cups frozen strawberries
- 3 tablespoons almond butter
- 1 cup almond milk
- 1 tablespoon flax seeds

Carrot Cake Shake:

- 1 scoop protein powder
- 1 frozen banana
- 1 cup frozen peaches
- 1 cup almond milk
- 4 medium carrots
- 1/2 teaspoon cinnamon
- 1/4 teaspoon nutmeg
- 1 tablespoon date sugar
- 4 tablespoons shredded coconut

Herbal Remedies:

Endometriosis is a disease that has affected women of all cultures and backgrounds for centuries. Before modern medicine and the pharmaceutical industry, each culture had its own herbal remedies and treatments that could be found in nature. The use of plants for healing purposes predates written history. Much of developed modern pharmaceuticals have roots in natural herbal remedies. For example, the active ingredient in aspirin is found in willow bark, opioid pain killers from the poppy plant, or penicillin from mold.

One way that herbal medicines differ from traditional pharmaceuticals is that many times herbal remedies will be made using the whole unpurified plant, or unpurified plant extracts, instead of just isolating the active ingredients. This way the person can gain the beneficial effects of the plant as a whole and not just one ingredient.

Often times herbal medicines will be created by mixing together more than one herb, to offer better results. This is a stark contrast to traditional pharmacology where in many cases it can be dangerous or harmful to mix medications.

Those who practice herbal medicine also tend to take a more holistic approach to diagnosis and treatment. In many cases they will try to look at the root cause of the problem, as well as recognizing general imbalances in the body which could lead to health problems. Health care professionals prescribing traditional pharmaceuticals are oftentimes only treating the symptoms.

With the ability to now ship and receive products worldwide it is possible to try a variety of herbal remedies from around the world, without living in the place where the plant is grown.

Listed below are some popular herbal remedies and supplements for those suffering with endometriosis.

Turmeric - beyond being just a tasty spice, turmeric also contains curcumin, which has anti-inflammatory properties, hormone regulating abilities, and antioxidant properties.

Aloe vera juice - the juice from the aloe vera succulent plant contains multiple vitamins including A, C, E, B1, B2, B3, B6, folic acid, and choline. Calcium, magnesium, zinc, selenium, iron, potassium, and manganese are also found in aloe vera juice. It is also high in amino acids and beneficial fatty acids, as well as being a powerful anti-inflammatory. If you decide to try aloe vera juice to get your vitamins, make sure you buy organic juice with no added sugars.

Ginger root powder - Ginger root powder taken daily has been shown to help manage pain in an equivalent fashion to ibuprofen.

Chaste Tree - the chaste tree is native to the Mediterranean region and has traditionally been used as a treatment for estrogen imbalances in women. Taking chaste supplements can help stimulate progesterone and treat menstrual cycle pain and premenstrual syndrome.

Rosemary - has been used for a long time as an anti-inflammatory and for pain relief.

Chamomile - according to some studies chamomile can reduce the symptoms of premenstrual syndrome as well suppress the growth of endometrial cells. Chamomile can be taken either in supplement form or consumed as a tea.

Peppermint - studies have shown that peppermint has antioxidant properties and can reduce pelvic pain and menstrual cramping.

Pine bark - there is some evidence that pine bark supplements can also help with inflammation.

Evening primrose oil - primrose oil extract contains gamma linolenic acid, which can help with symptoms of hormonal imbalance and stress. Primrose oil should not be taken if you have a history of seizures, are taking anticoagulants, or are on anti-psychotic medicine.

Milk Thistle - the seeds of milk thistle are anti-inflammatory in nature and support healthy liver function.

Asparagus extract - good for helping kidney function.

Pycnogenol - also known as French Maritime Pine Bark can help reduce excess estrogen. It is also a powerful antioxidant.

Dandelion root - helps to detoxify the liver and can also increase protein and fat uptake which can help with endometriosis symptoms.

Endometriosis and TCM (Traditional Chinese Medicine)

Traditional Chinese Medicine, a combination of various treatments and practices that have developed in China over thousands of years, has recently become popular in countries outside of China. When traditional western medicine does not provide relief many western women with endometriosis have started turning to TCM to help alleviate their pain and symptoms. TCM practitioners have a very holistic approach to treating conditions, by using a combination of mind and body practices, and herbal medicines and foods.

Acupuncture and **Tai Chi** are both common practices in TCM in general and can also be advised to treat endometriosis symptoms. **Acupuncture** is the stimulation of specific points in the body via the insertion of thin needles into the skin. It is believed that this stimulation affects the way the brain processes pain, releasing endorphins, and stimulating the body's release of natural painkillers. It is also suggested to promote blood circulation, regulate hormones, and have an anti-inflammatory effect. A study from the Nanjing Traditional Chinese Medicine University and Haian Traditional Chinese Medicine Hospital found that when comparing two groups of patients, one group being treated with acupuncture and traditional herbs, and the other being treated a progesterone-inhibiting synthetic steroid; the pain and symptom reduction were equivalent.

The two primary "acupoints", or points targeted by the acupuncture in the study were the "Zhongji" and "Zunsanli" acupoints. The "Zhongji" point is located just above the pubic symphysis and is believed to be the "moving and cooling point for endometrial disorders" by TCM practitioners. Activating the "Zhongji" point is believed to regulate blood and the "qi" of the uterus, causing a clearing and nourishing effect. [20]

The "Zunsanli" acupoint is located next to the anterior border of the tibia. This acupoint is believed to stimulate the regeneration of "yuan qi" which is proposed to activate the body's natural healing abilities. It is also believed to help with PMS, depression, nervousness, insomnia.[20]

Another common acupuncture point for endometriosis is the ear. [21, 22] There are dozens of acupuncture points on the ear that affect areas throughout the body. A study from The Journal of Traditional Chinese Medicine was performed on 67 women diagnosed with dysmenorrhea due to endometriosis. Half of the women received ear acupuncture whilst the other half did not. In the group of women that did receive acupuncture; 81% of them had less pain following the treatment. [21]

Tai Chi is a physical practice that is a common aspect of Traditional Chinese Medicine. It is a form of light exercise that combines gentle movements, breathing and postures, and mental relaxation techniques. Tai chi can be beneficial for women with endometriosis as it helps relieve tension, improve circulation, and increase energy levels. Many stances in Tai chi increase the flexibility and opening of the pelvic area. This is believed to allow energy to flow to those areas and stimulate the flow of the lymphatic system to reduce blood stagnation. It is also believed to reduce the development of cysts and fibroids within the pelvic area. [23]

Since Tai chi involves very gentle, slow movements, it is also a great way for women with endometriosis pain to get exercise and stretch. Unlike other more vigorous form of exercise, it can be a lot gentler on the body, and easier to perform for people with chronic pain. Since Tai chi also incorporates meditation and breathing regulation into the movements, it is excellent for reducing stress and anxiety, which many women with endometriosis suffer from. [23]

Traditional Chinese Medicine is generally much more individualized than western medicine. When visiting a practitioner of TCM, they will tailor your exact treatment plan and medicines to your condition and symptoms. It is rare for any two treatment plans to be exactly the same.

In a study from Taiwan of 3,219 women with endometriosis, treated from 1998-2008, the ten **herbal formulas** most commonly prescribed by TCM practitioners were the following: [24]

Gui-Zhi-Fu-Ling-Wan- **Cinnamon Twig and Poria Pill**

Dang-Gui-Shao-Yao-San - **Tangkuei and Peony Powder**

Jia-Wei-Xiao-Yao-San- **Augmented Rambling Powder**

Shao-Fu-Zhu-Yu-Tang- **Fennel Seed and Corydalis Combination**

Wen-Jing-Tang- **Tangkuei and Evodia Combination**

Shao-Yao-Gan-Cao-Tang - **Peony and Licorice Combination**

Long-Dan-Xie-Gan-Tang- **Gentiana Combination**

Xiao-Yao-San- **Rambling Powder**

Qui-Pi-Tang- **Ginseng and Longan Combination**

Xue-Fu-Zhu-Yu-Tang- **Persica and Carthamus Combination**

Each of these combinations contained at least one herb with an: antiproliferative effect, a sedative effect, an antioxidant effect, and an anti-inflammatory effect. The herbs are said to prevent blood stasis in the lower abdomen, relieve pelvic pain, regulate the menstrual cycle, ease breast swelling and tenderness, and treat many other symptoms of endometriosis.

Traditional Chinese Medicine is very common in Taiwan and has been practiced for hundreds of years. The study revealed that more than 90.8% of endometriosis patients in the country tried TCM at least once. [24]

Some have suggested that Traditional Chinese herbal medicines might provide symptom relief purely as a result of the placebo effect: However, clinical studies have shown that many Chinese herbs have sedative and pain-alleviating properties. [24]

Even ancient remedies that are less common in the modern age, such as red deer antler, which was used to treat male impotence and gynecologic disorders in women, have scientific evidence backing them. A recent animal study from an alternative medicine journal showed products made from antler velvet may "produce anti-inflammatory compounds that assist in the regulation of prostaglandins" (those hormones that are involved in pain and cramping).[8]

Some of the more obscure herbs listed above may be difficult to find outside of China. Herbs such as myrrh, cinnamon, ginger, gardenia, turmeric, red sage, red peony, gardenia, cardamom, cayenne Pepper, and saffron might sound more familiar and are all also herbs used in Traditional Chinese Medicine treatment of endometriosis.

Exercise and Endometriosis:

Exercise is a key part of holistic health, and essential to living a healthy life. Exercise is also particularly beneficial to women with endometriosis. As we know, endometriosis is related to a high amount of estrogen. Regular exercise can reduce your estrogen levels, helping to alleviate endometriosis symptoms. It can also help offset some of the physical damage done by endometriosis. The scar tissue and adhesions, that develop in some women with endometriosis, and that can bind tissues and organs together, can cause pain and make it hard to move. Exercising can strengthen the pelvic floor and the muscles around the bladder, vagina, and bowels. A study in the *Journal of Physical Therapy Science* showed that women who undertook an exercise plan that targeted the pelvic floor with a physical therapist experience significant decrease in pain.[25]

Exercise can also boost your mood, and reduce pain, by the release of something called endorphins. Endorphins act almost like a natural morphine released by your body! They affect the receptors in your brain that reduce your perception of pain, while also inducing a general positive feeling. Regular exercise will improve your overall mood, help you relax, and is even attributed to helping lower symptoms of depression and anxiety.

One thing to remember while exercising though: **do not overdo it**. Over exercising, as well as certain types of exercises can make endometriosis symptoms worse. Sit-ups, crunches, or even some high intensity cardiovascular exercise like running can make cramping worse, especially if you are already in pain. The key is just to pay attention to your body. Sometimes when it comes to exercise, we can have a "no pain, no gain" mentality and push ourselves beyond what is healthy. Some moderate amount of muscle soreness is good, but legitimate pain of any sort is not. If you are in pain, stop! Not every form of exercise is good for every person. If you feel that something is making your symptoms worse, you do not have to continue doing it. Find other forms of exercise that you enjoy, and that do not cause you pain.

Your exercise plan will vary based on your abilities and your symptoms and levels of pain. What one woman might be able to do with no problems might cause another excruciating pain. If you cannot do something, do not worry. Everyone has different capabilities.

Another thing to keep in mind is when it comes to exercise, try to enjoy it! Exercise should not be a chore, or something you dread doing. Try to make it fun! Maybe you like going to the gym! If so, great! If not, maybe try to get some of your exercise outside, worked into your daily life. Or do an activity you enjoy that gets you active. Go hiking, throw a frisbee with your family, sign up for an adult ballet class. The possibilities are endless.

Having endometriosis can be exhausting. Somedays you will not be able to exercise at all, and that is okay! Do what you can do, and just remember, something is better than nothing. You do not have to be an amazing athlete, or have washboard abs. The point of exercise is to make your body and mind feel the best they can. Do what feels right for you, even if you have to take it slowly. Build up your fitness level gradually. If you have never run more than a few blocks you are not going to be doing a marathon in a week!

Some good potential exercises for someone with endometriosis include:

Walking/Hiking - running can be too intense for some women with endometriosis, so taking a walk or a hike can be a great low-impact way of getting aerobic exercise.

Swimming/Water Aerobics - swimming is another great way of getting aerobic exercise with absolutely none of the impact that comes with running, since you are in the water. Water aerobics is a form of exercise, generally in a group setting, that involves a series of aerobic and resistance exercises while immersed in the water.

Bicycling - leisurely riding a bicycle can also be a great form of exercise. Some women do have trouble riding an upright bicycle and find that it does cause some pain but have found that riding what is called a reclined bicycle does not offer the same problems.

Yoga - many women with endometriosis find yoga to be beneficial for both their minds and their bodies. Yoga is a combination of physical, mental, and spiritual practices that developed in ancient India. Many people in the western world today practice it just as a form of exercise, but the meditation aspects can also be beneficial for coping with stress resulting from endometriosis.

Pilates - Pilates is a more recently develop form of exercise which focuses on controlled movements, which aim to improve flexibility, builds strength, and enhance overall endurance in the body. Much like yoga it focuses on both mental and physical health. Pilates can be helpful for strengthening muscles and reducing muscle pain and teneness associated with endometriosis.

Tai Chi - as mentioned before, Tai Chi is commonly part of a Traditional Chinese Medicine approach to treating endometriosis. The form of exercise is slow and gentle and is believed to help clear up the negative effects of blood stagnation.

Dancing - light, relaxed dancing, like ballroom dancing, or beginner ballet, can be a fun way to get some exercise and stretching in.

In addition to the general forms of exercise listed above, a woman with endometriosis might want to try focused exercise to strengthen and relax the muscles in and near the pelvis. Some examples of such exercises are below:

Side lying leg raises: Lie down on your side on a mat or the floor. Keep your body in a straight line with your feet stacked on top of each other. Put your arm under your head for support. You can either place your other arm in front of you or on your leg. Breathe out and gently raise the leg on top while keeping the bottom leg on the floor. Lower your leg slowly and repeat 10-15 times before switching to the other side.

Pelvic floor relaxation: the pelvic floor relaxation exercise can be described as a reverse Kegel. To do this exercise requires diaphragmatic breathing and concentration. Start by placing a hand on your chest, and your other hand on your abdomen right below your rib cage. Breathe in deeply for three seconds, and then exhale slowly on the fourth count. Try to relax and open your pelvic muscles, the same muscles you tighten to control your bladder, on the exhale.

Hip stretch: for this stretch lay on a mat or the floor with both knees bent. Then take one ankle and rest it on the opposite knee. Use your hand to gently press at the knee, stretching and opening your hips and pelvis. You can hold this stretch for up to a minute and repeat five times before switching sides.

Hip Flexor stretch: kneel on a mat or the floor, and then take a step forward with one foot, into a lunge. Bring arms up towards the ceiling and stretch. You can also hold this stretch for up to a minute.

Groin stretch: once again lay on a mat or the floor with both knees bent. Then slowly bring both knees up towards your chest and apart towards your shoulders. You can keep this position for up to a minute and then repeat five times.

Child's pose stretch: sit back on your heels on a mat or the floor. Curl forwards, bringing your forehead to the ground. Stretch your arms out in front of you. You can open your knees slightly as well to deepen the stretch. As you breath this stretch will help lengthen the pelvic floor. You can stay in this pose as long as it feels comfortable for you.

Horse stance stretch: stand upright with your feet slightly past shoulder-width apart. Straighten your shoulders and back. Bend your knees slowly and lower your upper body as if you were sitting on horseback. Make sure to keep your toes facing forward. You can stay in this stance as long as it is comfortable, but it will probably make your upper thighs burn after a while!

Butterfly stretch: sit on the floor with your knees out and the soles of your feet pressed together. Elongate and straighten your spine while tucking your chin and pressing gently down on your knees.

There are many exercises that could be helpful for women with endometriosis. Again, remember to stick with what works for you!

Part Three: Cultivating a better life with endometriosis

Lifestyle changes:

Hearing the words "lifestyle change" can be alarming. You might be pretty used to doing things the way you have been. Change can be scary, and the idea of making fundamental changes to your way of life can be intimidating. However, to fight your endometriosis symptoms and cure yourself to the best of your ability, change is necessary.

Stress and endometriosis:

Stress, without a doubt, can make any chronic health condition worse. Long-term constant stress can have very harmful effects. Short-term, small doses of stress or fear can be good. If you are in a dangerous situation you want stress to help motivate you to get out of the situation! However, our bodies are not built to process persistent, chronic stress. That kind of stress is neither productive nor helpful.

Chronic stress can worsen depression and anxiety. It can make it hard to sleep and give you headaches and stomach pains. It can affect your memory and ability to process information.

Over time stress physically wears on your body, affecting almost every organ system from your respiratory and cardiovascular systems to your reproductive system.

Sometimes it can be difficult to not feel stressed when you are suffering from endometriosis, especially when you are in constant pain. "Destressing" can seem impossible. Stress can be caused by a lot of things. However we might have other things in our life that are stressing us, of which we are not even aware. Work, relationships, family, finances, and more can all cause stress.

Uncertainty and not feeling like you are in control also lead to stress. While you cannot control everything in your life, taking control of things you can, will help to reduce your stress levels substantially.

As mentioned before **exercise** is wonderful for reducing stress. Exercise lowers your body's stress hormones such as cortisol. Develop an exercise routine you enjoy and make it a point to stick to it.

Consider taking **supplements** to manage stress. If your stress is particularly bad there are some herbal supplements commonly taken to help relieve stress. Some of them include:

Ashwagandha - an Ayurvedic herb, also known as "Indian Ginseng," can be used to treat stress and anxiety.

Green tea - while green tea does contain a small amount of caffeine, some studies also show that it might lower stress by boosting serotonin levels. Green tea also contains antioxidants which provide many health benefits.

Valerian root - a plant native to Europe and parts of Asia, medicine made from the root is colloquially known as "nature's Valium." Commonly used as a sleep aid for those suffering from insomnia, it can also be helpful for managing stress and anxiety.

Rhodiola rosea - a plant native to Russia that naturally stimulates the body's resistance to stress. It can help people suffering from burnout and chronic stress.

Kava kava - a psychoactive pepper that is traditionally made into a tea. It has a long history of being used ceremonially and to treat different medical conditions. It has a calming, euphoric effect.

Melatonin - if you have trouble sleeping at night because of stress, melatonin can help. Your body produces melatonin natural, but sometimes our melatonin levels can become imbalanced, leading to sleep problems. Blue and green light from electronic devices used right before bed can neutralize melatonin's effects because your brain associates bright light with daytime. High levels of stress can also affect melatonin production, leading to insomnia. Melatonin supplements can be taken at night to help you get to sleep more easily.

Phosphatidylserine - phosphatidylserine also occurs naturally in the body. It is a phospholipid that plays an important role in brain health and mental acuity. Phosphatidylserine supplements have been shown to counteract physical and mental effects of stress. It is best taken at bedtime.

L-Tyrosine - this is an amino acid synthesized in the body and found in foods such as meat, fish, dairy, eggs, nuts, and beans. L-Tyrosine supplements have been shown to help reverse mental decline and improve cognitive abilities in high-stress situations.

Glycine - glycine is another supplement that can help you get a good night's sleep. Glycine is an amino acid that stimulates the production of serotonin. It also has calming effects on the brain and is capable of lowering your core body temperature. Glycine is found in protein rich foods such as meat, poultry, fish, dairy, and legumes. It can also be taken in supplement form.

B-Complex - b-complex supplements contain all eight essential B vitamins: Vitamin B1, also known as thiamin, Vitamin B2, also known as riboflavin, Vitamin B3, also known as niacin, pantothenic acid, Vitamin B6, Vitamin b7, also known as biotin, and folate and folic acid. B vitamins help lower blood levels of an amino acid called homocysteine that is associated with stress. Those who have sufficient B vitamin levels will usually see a general improvement in mood and energy levels as well as less symptoms of stress such as anger, fatigue, and depression.

Foods that include B vitamins are meat, poultry, fish, nuts, legumes, eggs, and spinach. However, many people do not meet their B vitamin requirements through diet alone. Many people are in fact, B vitamin deficient, so taking supplements is a good idea.

Zinc - zinc is an essential mineral that is lacking in a lot of modern processed foods and modern diets. Zinc plays a role in modulating the brain and body's response to stress and deficiencies can lead to higher levels of stress, anxiety, and depression. At least three hundred enzymes in our bodies use zinc to help them perform their functions. Taking daily zinc supplements can help reduce stress and improve overall mental health.

Always consult with an expert before taking a new supplement. Especially if you are already taking several supplements, you want to make sure there will not be any negative interactions between the supplements.

Try **aromatherapy**, the use of natural plant extracts to promote health and well-being, usually either via the application of essential oils, or a candle or scent diffuser. Make sure to purchase pure, organic scents when possible. If you are using a candle you want to select one with few additives or possible irritants. Good scents for stress relief are the following:

> Lavender, Lemongrass, Lemon oil, Frankincense
> Peppermint, Rosemary, Eucalyptus, and Sage

Music therapy can help some people manage stress. Cheerful music can help stimulate the release of good endorphins, making you feel more optimistic and upbeat. Slow, relaxing music can have a soothing effect, and help relieve stress. Some cultures have traditional music meant to accompany meditation that can set a tranquil, relaxing mood.

Massage can also be excellent for helping relieve stress and tension. Stress can cause stiff, achy muscles, which massage helps remedy. Massage has been shown to have anti-inflammatory effects, give a euphoric effect, and increase serotonin and dopamine levels. If you are receiving a massage from a therapist or other person, you also benefit from the healing powers of human touch, which has been shown to decrease stress levels. Self-massage can also be beneficial, helping to loosen stiff muscles, and for encouraging awareness of one's own body.

Another good way to reduce stress is to **spend time in nature.** Being outside improves physical, emotional, and mental health. Humans are not adapted to the modern, urban environment. It has only been a few hundred years since the average person was living an agrarian life and spending much of their time outside and active. Now many people in the modern western world spend their days inside, sitting down, and hunching over a computer screen. Taking a break and getting outside into nature is restorative and soothing to the mind.

A study from the psychology department of Cornell University showed that as little as 10 minutes of time spent in nature daily was sufficient to reap positive benefits. The study revealed that daily time in nature resulted in an improved mood, better ability to focus, and even better physical characteristics such as blood pressure and heart rate.[26]

So, put your phone away, take a walk in the park. Start a porch garden. Play outside with your pets or children. Sit outside and read a book. There are a lot of possibilities.

Also make a point each week to **take some "me time"**. Develop and maintain **stress-relief routines**. Make time for leisure activities and hobbies that you enjoy, whether that is reading, kayaking, art, knitting, crossword puzzles, birdwatching, or anything else that brings you joy. At the end of the day try to have a relaxing routine. Take a hot bath or shower, read a book, watch a favorite show. Change into your favorite comfy clothes. Especially if you have a demanding family or work life, make sure you have solo time when you need it.

As part of your "me time," **pamper yourself.** Take a bubble bath, paint your nails, treat yourself to a pedicure, do a face mask, buy special "fancy" lotion. Do something that makes you feel good, inside, and out.

Look and feel the best you can. What makes you look and feel your best will probably change from a day to day basis and will vary depending on the person. One day you might feel your best in a fancy dress and heels. Another day it might be your softest, coziest pair of sweatpants. Either way, only wear things that you feel good in. Life is too short to wear uncomfortable clothes. There is plenty of discomfort to be had without adding to it.

Another aspect of looking and feeling your best is to keep up your hygiene. Wash your face, brush your teeth, invest in body care products that make you feel good. Make sure to shower or bathe daily. It is amazing how much better be clean can make you feel.

Try to get more, quality **sleep**. Sleep deprivation is a big cause of stress and anxiety. Your brain cannot function properly if you are not rested. Develop healthy sleep habits. Be consistent about the time you go to sleep and get up. Try not to stay up to late or sleep in too much on the weekends. Avoid large meals right before bed. Keep your room dark and at a comfortable temperature.

Make sure you do not bring work to bed. Once you are in bed you are done for the day. Do not answer emails or catch up on work on your laptop. If you are anxious about remembering to do something it is a good idea to keep a notepad by your bed so you can write down ideas and reminders for later.

Try to put up all electronics at least thirty minutes before you go to bed. Yes, that includes your cell phone! Even if you use your cellphone as an alarm clock, try to put it on nighttime mode and avoid scrolling through social media right before you go to sleep. Try reading or listening to an audiobook before bed to relax instead. If you want to watch a movie or show, or read on an electronic device, investing in a pair of anti-blue light glasses might be a good idea.

To reduce stress, try to **simplify your life** as much as possible. You might have heard the saying "a cluttered life means a cluttered mind." Having visual clutter can trigger the parts of the brain that relate to stress.

Keeping organized and clutter free can be very hard when dealing with a chronic health condition. Sometimes you just do not have any energy or ability to clean your house. A good strategy is just to take 10-15 minutes each day, whenever you can, and try to go through one section of your home that is cluttered. Try to sell or give away things that you do not really need, or things that do not make you happy. If you have an article of clothing for example that you have never worn once, do not keep it around just because you "might wear it one day." You probably will not.

Once you have minimized what you own, keep things less cluttered by following the "five-minute rule." If something can be done in five minutes, and you are able to do it, do not put it off. Wash the dishes now, fold your clothes and put them away. Not having visual reminders of chores that you have procrastinated will help reduce subconscious stress.

Another important thing to do to reduce stress, and what might be the most difficult thing of all is to **cut out negative people.** Every relationship will have its ups and downs. If you know someone for long enough, they will be eventually let you down or hurt you at some point, even if it is unintentional. The key to a healthy relationship is how you move on and make things right with each other. However, sometimes you will find yourself in a relationship that can only be described as toxic. Remember: it is not your responsibility to save other people. Everyone has issues and problems. A good friend will support you and be there for you in your tough times, just as you are for them. If you find yourself acting as an "emotion dump" for the other person all the time, and they are never there for you when you need it, you might need to consider the fact that the relationship could be toxic. If the other person always complains, and never has anything good to say, the relationship could be toxic.

If a person manipulates you, makes you feel bad about yourself, or emotional or physically abuses you in any way, you need to cut them out of your life. This can be incredibly hard to do, especially if its someone you have known for a long time, or even someone that is a member of your family. Just remember, there are many people who have gone through the same thing, and many support groups and other organizations that can help you. It may be hard at first, but your life will be much better in the long run.

Overextending and overcommitting yourself are two other factors that can lead to serious stress. **Learn how to say no.** Everyone needs downtime. While it is good to want to help other people and giving and volunteering to others can actually decrease stress and make us feel good about ourselves, there is a limit. You cannot truly be there for others if you are not taking care of yourself. Sometimes the best thing you can do is say no. People that are truly your friends and care for you will understand when you need time off. As a person with a chronic health condition, you need even more time to relax than the average person would. Do not push yourself too hard. That only leads to burnout.

Smoking and endometriosis:

Smoking nicotine is incredibly addictive and can be very difficult to quit. However, if you suffer from endometriosis it can make your symptoms and overall health much worse. Women who smoke experience have more severe premenstrual symptoms and cramps. Many of the chemicals included in tobacco today are also very inflammatory, which is terrible for endometriosis. They also cause cell damage over time, making it very hard for the body to heal itself.

Smoking in women is also known to cause complications with pregnancy and fertility. It is known to cause ectopic pregnancy.[59] Ectopic pregnancy is a condition in which the fertilized egg fails to move to the uterus, or womb, and instead attaches to other organs outside the womb. Women with endometriosis already have an increased risk of ectopic pregnancy.[60] So, for a woman with endometriosis that is attempting to get pregnant, it is especially recommended that they cease smoking.

Alcohol and endometriosis:

As covered previously in the diet section, alcohol and endometriosis do not mix. Alcohol raises estrogen levels, leading to worse endometriosis symptoms. Unfortunately, if you suffer with endometriosis you just cannot afford to go out and party every weekend without consequences. However, that does not mean you have to be a complete teetotaler. Some doctors say that it is okay to have an alcoholic drink occasionally, just infrequently, and no more than one in a day. If you do have a drink, red wine might be a good choice. Some evidence suggests that resveratrol, a compound present in red wine can have anti-estrogen effects. However, you would probably have to drink a ridiculous amount to see any real results, and the negative effects of the alcohol consumed would outweigh that. So, even if you are having red wine, still stick to one glass.

Non-alcoholic spirits and wine-alternatives are also becoming increasingly popular with health-conscious women. Many people enjoy the taste of certain types of alcohol, as well as the social aspect of having a drink, but do not want the negative side affects that come with consuming alcohol. Some non-alcoholic spirts even have herbal components that offer relaxing effects without the damage, or hangover.

Drink more water:

Really? You might be thinking. Of course, you know you should be drinking lots of water. It is said as a tip for dealing with almost everything, from helping your digestive system to getting clear skin. However, staying hydrated is especially important for someone with endometriosis.

Many women with endometriosis can suffer from constipation. Constipation can lead to toxicity in the body and store up of waste products and excess hormones such as estrogen. A healthy, regular gastrointestinal tract is essential for managing endometriosis symptoms. Being properly hydrated helps reduced constipation, thus allowing for better elimination of toxins through our daily bowel movements. Toxins are also released through the urine, and drinking more water means you will produce more urine, and thus flush out toxins and hormones more frequently.

You do not want to overdrink water obviously. Though rare, water toxicity is a thing. So how do you know exactly how much water you should be drinking a day? You may have heard the blanket statement that you should drink eight 8-ounce glasses of water a day, equaling a total of 64 ounces of water. That is not quite true, however. Necessary water consumption will vary from person to person. One easy way to calculate how much water you should aim to drink is to take your weight in pounds and divide that in half. For example, if you weigh 130 pounds, you should try to drink 65 ounces of water a day.

Several ideas to remind yourself to drink more water are:

Make it a part of your routine- drink water when you wake up, along with a cup of coffee, with each meal, and before you go to bed at night.

Set alarms- set various alarms at set points throughout the day to remind yourself to drink water.

Carry a water bottle- invest in a good, sturdy, stainless steel, or glass water bottle. You can even get water bottles with measurement marks on the side. Try to avoid drinking out of plastic water bottles, which are full of toxins.

Make infused water- if you have trouble making yourself drink water, try to make it taste good! Add lemon or cucumber or other fruits and herbs.

Positive thinking:

Sometimes life with endometriosis can feel hopeless. The pain, the fatigue, and the isolation that the disease causes can all be absolutely draining. Always remember though, your illness does not define you. Despite all the misery it forces you to endure, endometriosis can change your outlook on life for the better. Endometriosis can make you an incredibly strong person. You can learn to appreciate things that others might take for granted. While endometriosis is something that you have all the time, it is not who you are. Some days will be better than others, but there will always be good days.

Avoiding Environmental Toxins:

In the modern, industrial world humans are exposed daily to more toxins than ever before in history. Every day we come into to contact with chemicals and ingredients that can disrupt our hormones, upset our biological systems, and even cause cancer. Many illness and health conditions are much more prevalent today than they ever were before. Things such as cancer, obesity, and mood disorders have always existed of course, but they are becoming much more common. There is evidence to suggest that this might be due to the large amount of environmental toxins present today.

One specific type of toxic chemical, called a xenoestrogen, is especially harmful for women with endometriosis. As we have covered, endometriosis is tied to an overabundance of estrogen in the body. What you might not know is that our environment and the things we consume actually cause us to have a harmful extra amount of estrogen. Xenoestrogens are synthetic chemicals that mimic estrogen, meaning they act just like extra estrogen would in the body.

Not only are xenoestrogens toxic to humans, but these pollutants tend to degrade slowly in the environment and bioaccumulate in the food chain. Once they make their way into humans, they have very long half-lives, meaning they can last a long time in the body.

Xenoestrogens are so prevalent in the world today, that they are even thought to be causing an epidemic of what is referred to as "precocious puberty." Essentially, as a result of xenoestrogens, more children are beginning puberty earlier than is natural or healthy.

Unfortunately, xenoestrogens are found in an alarming number of things we use or consume every day. They are found in plastic, cosmetics, in the pesticides used on produce, in cleaning products, in meat and dairy products, and many other places. It seems like xenoestrogens are almost everywhere, so how do you avoid them, or at least limit your exposure? Some ideas are listed below:

Get a filter for your water - scarily, xenoestrogens have even been found in tap water! Buying a water filter is a great way to reduce the amount of toxins you are getting in your drinking water.

Avoid GMOs - genetically modified foods were first developed in the 1990s as a way of producing better, heartier crops. However, GMOs have also been tied in with unhealthy estrogen regulation.

Buy organic - many pesticides used on non-organic crops have tons of harmful chemicals and pesticides, not limited to xenoestrogens that are associated with reproductive health problems in both women and men.

Only buy hormone-free meat - lots of industrial meat is now produced by pumping up the animals with massive amounts of hormones and antibiotics. Meat produced with hormones is a large contributor to xenoestrogens in the population.

Reduce plastic use - plastic is full of harmful xenoestrogens. Never microwave in plastic, even microwavable tv-dinners. Try to eliminate plastic Tupperware and Ziploc bags from your kitchen. Glass Tupperware containers are a great alternative. They are also easier to clean, and microwavable so you can eat straight out of them and save time doing dish, which is a plus!

Eat plenty of fiber - fiber, specifically cruciferous vegetables like cauliflower, cabbage, Brussels sprouts, broccoli, and kale actually help in removing excess estrogen from the body.

Avoid coffee - coffee has actually been shown to significantly increase estrogen levels in addition to excess caffeine not being good for endometriosis. Try to drink green or black tea instead.

Read cosmetic and personal product labels - your skin is your biggest organ. So many of the environmental toxins we are exposed to every day are absorbed through our skin, so you want to be careful what you put on it! Try to buy products that are all natural, or organic. Usually, the less ingredients the better. If you don't know what an ingredient is, look it up!

Some people might say that "if you cannot pronounce it, do not buy it!" That is not necessarily the best rule to follow though, as sometimes companies are intentionally confusing by using the scientific sounding name for every ingredient, so you cannot tell the bad from the good. Even water, scientifically known as dihydrogen monoxide, can sound scary if you do not know what it is. Some specific things to always avoid are listed below:

- **Parabens**
- **Methenamine**
- **Sodium hydroxy methyl glycinate**
- **Sodium Lauryl Sulfate and Sodium Lauretha Sulfate**
- **Petroleum**
- **Lead**
- **Phthalates**
- **Carbon black**
- **Formaldehyde**
- **Aluminum**
- **Siloxanes**

Only use organic sanitary product - only buy organic pads and tampons. It is especially crucial to use organic and bleach free tampons. Vaginal tissue is very absorbent, and there are lots of harmful chemicals and pesticides in regular tampons. A menstrual cup made from silicone can also be a good alternative to tampons and can be left in longer without risk of toxic shock syndrome. A menstrual cup can also be more cost effective in the long run. The average woman spends more than $6,000 in her lifetime on sanitary products!

Use organic cleaning products - household cleaning products are another huge source of environmental toxins. Organic or even homemade cleaning products are a good option. Some toxins to avoid in cleaning products are listed below:

- **Ammonia**
- **Chlorine**
- **Sodium Hydroxide**
- **Quaternary Ammonium Compounds**
- **Triclosan**
- **Phthalates**
- **2-Butoxyethanol**
- **Formaldehyde**
- **Perchloroethylene (PERC)**

Try to avoid hormonal birth control- there are many good reasons to take birth control pills, or other form of hormonal birth control. However, if you are only taking birth control to prevent pregnancy, and not for any medical reasons, you might want to reconsider. Using a barrier method may be just as effective and will not affect estrogen levels.

Buy BFR free furniture - BFRs or brominated flame-retardants contain xenoestrogens and are found in many types of furniture, mattresses, carpets, rugs, and even some electronics. Look for ecofriendly furniture companies that do not use chemical laden varnishes and finishes.

Avoid canned food - many canned foods have a plastic lining. Try to buy fresh food, or make sure you are buying canned food without the plastic lining.

Take off your shoes when you come inside - we step on a lot of things throughout our daily lives. There are a lot of nasty things on the street, including environmental toxins. Keep them out of your house as much as possible by taking off your shoes and putting on a pair of clean, indoor-only slippers.

Change air filters in house frequently - you should be changing the air filter in your house once every 90 days, or every 60 days if you have pets.

How to detoxify your body:

Sometimes with so many environmental toxins around us, our bodies can start to accumulate those toxins, and the effects become evident. Some signs you might need a detox include unusual fatigue and sluggishness, irritated skin and allergies, recurring infections, bloating, confusion, and general brain fog. To help your body detoxify on a daily basis make sure to:

Support your gut - to cleanse your gut and encourage good gut health try to eat things such as:

- Fermented foods like yogurt, kefir, sauerkraut, kimchi, miso, and kombucha.
- High fiber fruits and vegetables, and sprouts.
- Healthy fats such as salmon and tuna, nuts, seeds, olive oil, avocados, and coconut oil.
- Dairy-free milk such as almond, oat, or coconut milk.
- Herbs and spices such as ginger, garlic, cinnamon, and turmeric.
- Apple cider vinegar, tamari, and coconut aminos.
- Herbal tea.
- Foods with high water content such as watermelon, cantaloupe, lettuce, spinach cucumber, celery, and tomatoes.

Exercise - you might have heard the phrase "sweat it out" before. That's exactly what exercise helps us do! Exercise helps our lungs, kidneys, and other organ systems eliminate lots of bad toxins. It also encourages blood and lymph flow. Good workouts specifically aimed at detoxification are:

- Hot yoga
- Foam rolling
- Stretching
- Bodyweight exercises
- Any aerobic exercise

Other ways to detoxify are:

Sauna - sauna is a small room or building designed to get very hot for therapeutic purposes. "Saunas" themselves were historically from ancient Finland, but many cultures all around the world have sweat bathing traditions. Ancient Rome had the "Thermae," Turkey had the "Hammam," many Native American cultures had "Sweat Lodges," Russia had "banyas", Sweden had the "Batsu", Japan had the "Mushi-Buro", and Korea had the "Jjimjilbang." Sauna or sweat bathing helps to free toxins from adipose, or fat, tissue. Sauna can also help to free the body of viruses, bacteria, and other harmful microorganisms. It has also been associated with other health benefits such as stress relief, lower risk of heart attack, dementia and Alzheimer's, and longer lifespan.[28] You should build up your heat tolerance to the sauna by staying just a few minutes and then cooling off with a shower before going back in again. You also should not exceed 10 minutes in the sauna at any one time.

Infrared therapy - infrared therapy and infrared rooms are like a sauna but use infrared heaters to emit infrared light instead of traditional heated rocks or steam.

Dry-brushing - dry brushing an ancient practice that involves brushing dry skin with a natural-bristle brush. It helps to stimulate the lymphatic system and exfoliate your skin. Stimulating the lymphatic system helps with the detoxing process by removing cell waste, environmental toxins, and pathogens from your body. Dry brushing can also clear skin, make it smoother, reduce cellulite, and give you a boost of energy.[29] To dry-brush get a natural-bristled brush and brush your skin, starting from your feet, and brushing upward towards your heart in long, slow strokes.

Hydrotherapy - hydrotherapy involves alternating hot and cold water. This can be done in the shower by changing the water from hot to cold over several intervals.

Colon cleanse - a colon cleanse, or colonic should only be performed by an expert. During a colonic the practitioner streams water in the colon through the rectum. This is a way to rid your body of excess toxins that collect over time through eating and drinking. It can help with bloating, fatigue, weight gain, and skin problems.[30]

Drink a detox smoothie - make a smoothie with raw fruits and vegetables and probiotic foods such as kefir and yogurt. An easy to digest detox smoothie full of fiber and probiotics can help regulate your gastrointestinal tract and thus eliminate waste and toxins.

Activated charcoal - activated charcoal has been used since the 1800s for detoxing. It is carbon material that has been processed to contain many tiny pores that make it great for adsorption, or binding to toxins. Take activated charcoal at least 1 hour before and 2 hours after meals. Activated charcoal might also help with symptoms of irritable bowel syndrome such as diarrhea, gas, and bloating.[31] Check with your medical professional before using activated charcoal, as it can make some medications and supplements less effective. You also do not want to use activated charcoal too frequently because it can cause digestive blockages.

Cryotherapy - cryotherapy is a process where the body is subjecting to extreme cold for a short period of time, generally in a specially designed cold chamber. You go into the chamber from the neck down, where your body is safely exposed to nitrogen vapor. This process releases endorphins, causing an analgesic effect that reduces pain and swelling throughout the whole body. It also increases blood and lymph node circulation. [32]

Try short term fasting - even a short fast can help to eliminate toxins from your body. [33] Almost every religion has some sort of controlling fasting ritual, and for good reason! Make sure to drink plenty of water even while fasting, or the toxins will not be flushed out!

Ion-water detox - an ion-water detox, or ion-foot detox, pulls the toxins out of your body through your feet. An ionizing machine in a foot bath gives the hydrogen in the water a positive charge, which then attracts the negatively charged toxins in your body. [34]

Castor oil packs - applying castor oil packs to the abdomen is a good way stimulating the liver and colon. To make a castor oil pack, rub castor oil over skin, cover the area with an old towel and then apply a hot water bottle on top of the towel. You can leave the pack on for one hour or longer. This will allow the castor oil to reach the underlying organs under the area of the pack. The heat from the hot water bottle helps the castor oil penetrate the liver and intestines, which stimulates their contraction and encourages movement. This causes the release of toxins and waste. [35]

Epsom salt baths - Epsom salts, or magnesium sulfate salts help to pull out toxic build up, such as lactic acid build up, out from the muscles.[36] Make sure to drink plenty of water before and after an Epsom salt bath to further aid with toxins elimination.

Therapies and Treatments:

Today, when talking about therapies or treatments for endometriosis in a conventional medical setting, what will usually be brought up are things along the lines of hormonal therapies, or surgeries. As discussed earlier though, these are not your only options for relief! Other than the holistic medicines, foods, and lifestyles changes discussed earlier, there are other forms of non-invasive therapies and pain relief that also do not involve negative hormone altering prescription medicine.

TENS Electrotherapy:

One type of therapeutic treatment that can be used to manage endometriosis pain is something called TENS, which stands for transcutaneous electrical nerve stimulation, electrotherapy. A TENS unit is generally a small battery-operated device that applies light electrical impulses through electrodes. The electrodes have adhesive pads so the user can attach them to the area experiencing pain.

The idea behind the TENS unit is that the electrical impulses it emits will flood the nervous system and thus reduce its ability to transmit pain signals to the spinal cord and to be processed by the brain. The electrical impulses will also stimulate the body to produce its own natural pain relievers, endorphins.

TENS is a good, noninvasive way for many people to relieve pain. Some people who use TENS units for chronic pain can reduce the amount of pain medication they would otherwise normally take. They are also relatively inexpensive and can come in small, portable sizes, so they are easy to take with you wherever you go, in case you need quick access to pain relief. There are even some TENS units that are designed specifically for women with menstrual and endometriosis related pain.

There has not been much extensive research into TENS therapy for endometriosis, but many women with firsthand experience using TENS units find them incredibly helpful for pain management. One study from 2015 looked at 22 women with endometriosis who were already going through hormone therapy, but still had significant pelvic pain, and opted to use TENS devices to help treat paint. The study was over an 8-week period and found that the women had "significant improvement for chronic pelvic pain, deep dyspareunia, and quality of life by the use of TENS".

Shiatsu (acupressure):

Shiatsu is a type of massage originating in Japan, that works similarly to acupuncture, but without the needles. The word "Shiatsu" means finger pressure. Originally, it was mostly practiced in Japan, but began to become popular around the world starting in the 1950's. In 1964 the Japanese government officially declared both that Shiatsu was an independent method of treatment, as well as practicing Shiatsu to be a profession.

Just like acupuncture, Shiatsu or acupressure, is centered on certain pressure points in the body in order to relieve pain and symptoms. Massage therapy in general has been shown to help ease pain and associated feelings of stress. Shiatsu particularly has been connected to decreased endometriosis related pain.

A questionnaire given to university students in Iran found that in young women with endometriosis, acupressure significantly decreased their levels of pain. In fact, when compared to the results for taking ibuprofen regularly, it was shown to be more effective at reducing pain than the ibuprofen.[39] Unlike ibuprofen, acupressure does not have any significant side effects. Regular use of ibuprofen can lead to stomach upset and eventually damage over time. Acupressure is safe to perform even to oneself if you learn the pressure points to activate.

Shiatsu massage is frequently available from most trained masseuses. There are also some that specialize specifically in shiatsu for pain management. Some pain clinic doctors and chiropractors also use Shiatsu as a form of treatment.

Myofascial massage:

Myofascial massage or myofascial release is a type of physical therapy. It is often used to treat what is called myofascial pain syndrome. Myofascial pain syndrome is a chronic pain disorder that results from tension and tightness in myofascial tissue, that tissue which surrounds and supports the muscles throughout the body. Myofascial pain is very common in women with endometriosis, especially in the abdominal area. Studies have shown that manual manipulation can help to improve the tissue texture and mobility of the organs in areas affected by endometriosis. This can help to soften and remove adhesions. [67]

Not every physical therapist does myofascial massage. When looking for a physical therapist to do myofascial massage, it is also important to choose a therapist that has experience working with patients with endometriosis. Myofascial massage for endometriosis can also include treatment of the pelvic floor, which involves internal vaginal work. This is like a visit to the gynecologist. The therapist will use gloved and lubricated fingers to examine and treat the pelvic floor muscles and other internal structures. Obviously, if you opt for treatment of the pelvic floor you want to make sure that your therapist is someone you are comfortable with, and someone with which you have good communication.

Acupuncture:

As we covered previously, acupuncture is a common form of treatment in Traditional Chinese Medicine. According to Traditional Chinese Medicine, acupuncture works via balancing the qi, the energy or life force, and that balancing is what leads to the relief of pain and symptoms. Modern science attributes the success of acupuncture to the stimulation of muscles, nerves, and connective tissues. Either way, many women with endometriosis find acupuncture to be very helpful. It is natural, and less risky, and provides much fewer side effects than many other modern pain control methods.

If you decide to try acupuncture, definitely see a specialist. Unlike acupressure, you do not want to try it at home. It does involve the insertion of sharp objects into your body after all, so you are going to want someone who is trained and knows what they are doing! If you visit an acupuncture practitioner, you might also receive a Traditional Chinese Medicine diagnosis based on your own unique symptoms. The diagnosis will be used to develop an individualized acupuncture treatment plan for you.

Some people might find the idea of acupuncture inherently frightening. Sticking needles into your skin? That might not sound like a great way to relieve pain. However, most people describe acupuncture as a very relaxing experience. Unlike the needles used for getting shots, or drawing blood, acupuncture needles are very, very slim. Usually, they are not much larger than a strand of hair. You should not feel any pain with their insertion. Some patients fall asleep during acupuncture treatments.

Your acupuncturist will set up an exact treatment plan for you and tell you how frequently you will need to come in, but frequently patients will have an appointment approximately once a week or so. It may take several sessions before you start to feel any significant effects, so you do not want to just go once and then stop. Experts recommend going to at least 5 to 10 appointments.

The exact effectiveness of acupuncture for endometriosis in general still needs more study. However, several trials have showed promise, and many women have good personal experience with acupuncture. A 2014 study from Tongji University Hospital in Shanghai compared acupuncture with a standard synthetic steroid drug therapy. They found that not only was the acupuncture therapy effective, but it was more effective than the steroid therapy. The patients who received acupuncture had 92% total effective rate, whereas the steroid only had a 52% total effective rate. Follow ups also showed that the relapse rate for patients who received the acupuncture was less than for the patients that received the steroid therapy.
40

Cupping:

Cupping has increased in popularity in recent years. You have probably heard about the red, circular marks the practice causes, spotted on celebrities, from movie starts to Olympic athletes. But what exactly is cupping, and what are its benefits?

Cupping, like acupuncture, has its roots in traditional Chinese medicine. The practice was first documented almost 3,000 years ago. The practice of cupping involves the use of suction and heat to promote healing. The technique utilizes either bamboo jars or small glass cups that are heated before being placed directly on the skin. To heat them, the cups are sometimes brushed with rubbing alcohol and lit on fire, or they will be placed over a flame. The heat is not applied directly to the skin, so the practice will not result in any sort of burns. The heating of the cups or jars helps to eliminate oxygen and create a vacuum, which causes suction. When the cups are placed on the body, the practitioner can then glide the cups over the skin, bringing suction to any desired spot.

In addition to heated cupping, also known as dry cupping, there is also air cupping and wet cupping. Air cupping involves the use of a pump to create a vacuum. Wet cupping involves the slight puncturing of the skin, which results in a tiny amount of blood being sucked up into the cup. Wet cupping is believed to help clear toxins from the body through the blood.

However the vacuum is created, whether via heat, or an air pump; it will result in the skin being drawn up and into the glass. Depending on the condition, the cups may be left on the skin for up to 10 minutes. When the skin is sucked into the cup it causes the pores to open, the muscles to relax, and blood flow to improve. In Traditional Chinese Medicine cupping is also believed to remove toxins, balance the qi, and break up blockages. Just as with acupuncture, the cups are placed along "meridians" in the body. The most common area of the body to perform cupping is on the back, but cupping can also be performed on the legs, stomach, and arms.

Cupping is frequently performed as a general therapeutic treatment to improve overall health and body function, as well as to relax muscles. Many athletes use cupping as a way to aid in muscle recovery. However, the practice is also is thought to treat specific conditions as well. It is commonly used for respiratory issues, depression, swelling, gastrointestinal disorders, chronic back and neck pain, fatigue, migraines, and cellulite. Many women with endometriosis also use cupping to alleviate pain and muscle soreness caused by the condition.

Cupping is not appropriate or safe for everyone. If you practice cupping too frequently it can cause side effects such as persistent skin discoloration or scarring. If you have a skin condition such as eczema or psoriasis, it can worsen those conditions. If you do decide to try cupping therapy, you want to find a practitioner licensed in acupuncture or traditional Chinese medicine. The treatment is frequently used in conjunction with acupuncture therapy, and the two treatments can be alternated.

Heat therapy:

"Heat therapy" is a very broad term and can come in many different forms. It is generally considered a home remedy, as it can be practiced by methods such as taking a hot bath, using heating pads, water bottles, packs, or blankets, or other heating tools designed for pain relief.

We do not know the exact mechanism by which reduces endometriosis-related pain and cramping. However, heat is known to increase circulation, open up blood vessels, heal damaged tissue, relax muscles, and affect pain receptors in the body, all of which are potential pain-reducing properties.

The stomach, abdomen, pelvic floor, and lower back are all common areas of pain for women with endometriosis. Heating tools can be applied to any of these areas. The one thing to be cautious about is the level of heat, especially applied directly to the skin. You want to make sure you do not accidentally burn yourself, but other than that heat therapy is a very safe form of treatment. Many women with endometriosis will even invest in wireless heating packs so that they can take pain relief with them when not at home or near a power source.

Enzyme therapy:

Systemic enzyme therapy is growing in popularity as an effective natural therapy for endometriosis. So, what exactly is systemic enzyme therapy? Well, the word "systemic" indicates that something is body wide. Systemic enzymes are those that operate throughout your body in almost every organ and organ system. Systemic enzymes have been shown to aid in the breakdown of scar tissue and other extra tissues resulting from endometriosis. They have also been shown to aid in reducing inflammation caused by such scar tissue. Helping to reduce scar tissue and other adhesions has been directly linked to reducing pain from endometriosis. [41]

Studies of systemic enzyme therapy have showed that therapy results in significant positive effects such as reducing inflammation, aiding metabolism, and boosting the immune system. They have also been shown to significantly help with the healing process after injury or stress to the body.[42]

In the human body we have what are called macrophages. Macrophages are large phagocytic cells, cells that engulf other harmful cells or foreign particles. The word "macrophage" in Greek literally translated to "large eater." Generally, in a normally functioning human body the macrophages will "clean up" cellular debris and dead or dying cells. In a healthy woman, macrophages play an important role in the menstrual cycle. They help with tissue regeneration, the initiation of menstruation, and the clear up of endometrial tissue debris.

However, in a woman with endometriosis, the macrophages do not perform their functions in the proper way. One enzyme, called **Serrapeptase**, can digest dead tissue, blood clots, cysts, and plaque like normally functioning macrophages would. Serrapeptase is a naturally occurring enzyme that can be found in silkworms, where it is produced to help them breakdown their cocoons in the process of transforming into a moth. Since its discovery in silkworms, a way to produce it in the laboratory has been developed via a fermentation process.

Serrapeptase is capable of distinguishing between living and dead tissue and therefore will not harm living tissue, making it safe to take. There are no known side effects of Serrapeptase, though as with all medicine or supplements, it is good to start with small doses and make sure your body does not have any adverse reaction.

Serrapeptase is classified as a medicine and is commonly taken in Japan and many European countries for endometriosis, but also for a variety of conditions related to inflammation such as sinusitis, arthritis, fibromyalgia, carpal tunnel, Crohn's disease, and blood clots. In the U.S. however, it is classified as a dietary supplement and is less commonly taken or prescribed. Few doctors will mention or recommend Serrapeptase, so it frequently falls on the patient to do their own research and propose it as a treatment.

Nattokinase is another natural enzyme that works somewhat similarly to Serrapeptase. It is extracted from a fermented Japanese food known as Natto. Natto is made by the addition of the bacterium Bacillus natto to boiled soybeans. This results in the fermentation process, of which a natural byproduct is the enzyme Nattokinase.

Despite being produced from a soybean product, the enzyme of Nattokinase does not have any actual soybean in it. Therefore, for women with endometriosis that are worried about consuming soy products because of estrogen, Nattokinase is still perfectly fine to take.

Nattokinase has shown much promise for dealing with many different conditions, especially cardiovascular conditions. Specifically, Nattokinase has been proven to help with blood coagulation factors, thrombolysis, and hypertension.[42] Nattokinase functions by aiding in the breakdown and removal of "fibrins", insoluble proteins formed from fibrinogen during the clotting of blood, which form fibrous meshes. These fibrous meshes impede the flow of blood and fibrin adhesions might leads to menstruation in a retrograde manner, resulting in endometriosis. Taking Nattokinase might help remove, and prevent, fibrin adhesions from forming.

The enzyme also has a long history of safe human consumption. Nattokinase is widely used in Asian countries such as Japan, China, and Korea, and is also becoming popular in Australia, New Zealand, the United States, and Canada. The cost of Nattokinase supplements is also relatively inexpensive, especially when compared to most pharmaceutical medicines. [42]

Other popular over-the-counter enzyme supplements include **Bromelain, Papain, Trypsin,** and **Chymotrypsin.** [43] Bromelain is a type of enzyme found in the fruit and stem of the pineapple plant. Bromelain has been studied for both its anti-inflammation and swelling properties, as well as for pain relief. Bromelain is generally safe to take, however, it can have negative interactions with the antibiotic amoxicillin as well as with anticoagulant or antiplatelet drugs. If you are on any of the aforementioned medicines, make sure to speak with your healthcare professional before starting Bromelain supplementation. You can get Bromelain just from eating pineapple, but it is also available in supplement form.

Papain, also known as papaya proteinase, is an enzyme that can be found in papaya fruit. Just like Bromelain can be acquired from eating pineapple, papain can be acquired from eating raw papaya fruit. It is also available in topical, chewable, and swallowable capsule form. Some supplement companies even sell Papain/Bromelain supplement combinations that can be taken in one capsule or tablet. Papain is believed to ease pain, aid in wound healing, and reduce inflammation. It is also a beneficial enzyme for digestive health, and can help reduce symptoms of constipation and bloating, both of which are common among women with endometriosis.

Trypsin is another enzyme that helps the body to break down protein. It is also beneficial for digestion, as well as having anti-inflammatory effects. Trypsin is naturally produced in the human body in the pancreas, but certain conditions such as malabsorption can lead to a lack of the enzyme. Trypsin can also be made outside the human body in fungus, plants, and bacteria. Supplements are available generally in tablet form or as a topical cream.

Chymotrypsin is another digestive enzyme normally produced by the pancreas. It is converted into its active, or functioning form, by Trypsin. Chymotrypsin supplements can be taken by mouth as liquid "shots." They also sometimes come in inhalable form that is meant to be breathed in. Supplements are supposed to help with pain and swelling. Allergic reactions and anaphylaxis with Chymotrypsin supplementation is rare, but does occur, so check with your medical provider first.

Many women with endometriosis find Systemic Enzyme Therapy to be the missing piece to their endometriosis treatment plan. Systemic Enzyme Therapy can help improve pain and symptoms of endometriosis as well as physical cysts and abscesses. It can also generally improve health and wellbeing by aiding digestive health and helping to regulate the digestive processes that can be upset due to endometriosis.

Aromatase inhibitors:

Aromatase inhibitors are a type of hormonal treatment that helps to stop the production and overproduction of estrogen. They function by blocking the enzyme aromatase which is responsible for converting the hormone androgen into estrogen in the body. Pharmaceutical Aromatase inhibitors are frequently given to postmenopausal women suffering from breast cancer. This is because less estrogen results in less stimulation of the growth of hormone-receptor-positive breast cancer cells.

In recent years Aromatase inhibitors have also been identified as potential therapeutic treatments for endometriosis. In premenopausal women, aromatase is primarily found in the ovarian cells. Inhibiting aromatase will suppress estrogen synthesis in the ovaries and nearby tissues. As we have discussed before, endometriosis is linked to estrogen dominance, so by reducing the amount of estrogen produced in the body, it is possible to reduce symptoms and pain.

In normal human females, there is no aromatase at all in the endometrial tissue. However, in women with endometriosis there is notable aromatase activity. Aromatase activity stimulates estrogen production in the endometrial tissues, which in turn stimulates more aromatase activity which it should not be. It is a viscous cycle that taking Aromatase inhibitors can help to stop.

Many studies have researched the effectiveness of Aromatase inhibitors for women with endometriosis. They determined that Aromatase inhibitors were effective and that they decrease pain, reduce the size of endometrial lesions outside the uterus, and improve the overall quality of life in women with endometriosis.

Aromatase inhibitors have also been used as a treatment for infertility caused by endometriosis as well as Polycystic Ovarian Syndrome. Clinical trials have shown promise with using Aromatase inhibitors to induce ovulation, followed by intrauterine insemination.[45]

The three most commonly prescribed Aromatase inhibitors are chemically known as Anastrozole, Exemestane, and

Letrozole. Common brand names are Arimidex, Aromasin, and Femara. You will need a prescription for any of the above Aromatase inhibitors. However, there are natural estrogen blocking supplements that do not require a prescription.

Natural estrogen blockers include:

Wild nettle root: wild nettle root has been historically used as a natural prostate medication. This is due to compounds in the root that act as natural estrogen blockers. Women with endometriosis made the connection and have realized that it can be a beneficial supplement for their condition as well. Nettle also contains compounds that reduce inflammation and interfere with the body's processing of pain.

Chrysin: chrysin is a compound found naturally in both honey and passionfruit. It is believed to lower estrogen levels and increase testosterone levels. Obviously, you can add more honey and passionfruit to your diet, but to get substantial amounts of chrysin you will need to take a supplement. The concentrated form found in most supplements is extracted from the compound in passion flowers.

Indole-3-Carbinole (I_3C): I3C is a resulting compound that comes from consuming cruciferous vegetables such as Brussels sprouts, cabbage, cauliflower, broccoli, and kale. I3C is known to stimulate detoxifying enzymes in the gut and liver. It also regulates estrogen activity and metabolism.

Diindolylmethane (DIM): Diindolylmethane is a compound derived from the digestion of indole-3-carbinol. DIM supports estrogen balance by increasing beneficial estrogens and reducing the unwanted estrogens, which improves overall estrogen metabolism and helps to resolve estrogen dominance.[68]

Maca: maca root is a cruciferous plant that is originally native to Peru, where it is used both for food and for medicinal purposes. It has been scientifically proven to help lower overly high estrogen levels and restore hormonal balance in the body.[46] Maca root supplements have become increasingly popular, and readily available in the western world in recent years. Other benefits include boosting energy, improving mood, helping memory, increasing fertility, and promoting natural antioxidants in the body.

Myomin: Myomin is a Chinese herb combination that promotes proper hormonal balance. Similar to DIM, it also helps to metabolize excess estrogens, and inhibits aromatase.

Calcium D-Glucarate: Calcium D-glucarate aids in detoxification by eliminating hormones from the body. It helps prevent buildup of estrogen by inhibiting an enzyme in the intestine, beta-glucaronidase. When beta-glucaronidase encounters a hormone just as estrogen that has been neutralized, it can break the bond in the hormone to reactivate it and allow for reabsorption through the wall of the intestine. Calcium D-glucarate, stops this from occurring and by inhibiting beta-glucaronidase it makes sure that that the hormone will be excreted from the body and not reabsorbed. This prevents too many hormones from being reabsorbed and makes sure that if your body does not need a certain hormone at that time, such as estrogen, it will be excreted.

Grape seed extract: grapes and grape seeds contain procyanidins, which are a type of flavonoid that act very similar to pharmaceutical aromatase inhibitors. Grape seed oil is actually a natural byproduct of the wine-making industry and can be purchased for cooking use. The oil is high in beneficial Omega-6 Fatty Acids which can decrease inflammation as well. Other than the oil form, grape seed extract is also available in supplement form.

Long term use of pharmaceutical Aromatase inhibitors has been linked with increased risk of osteoporosis and bone fractures, so this might be a concern for older women or women with pre-existing osteoporosis. If you are concerned about how Aromatase inhibitors or estrogen blockers might affect your bone health, talk to your healthcare professionally before including them in your treatment plan.

Progesterone cream:

As we have talked about previously, endometriosis is closely linked to estrogen dominance. Both and progesterone and estrogen are key hormones, however, they must remain at a ratio of 30:1 in the body. When they fall outside that range, there is an imbalance.

We have already discussed some of the ways to increase progesterone and decrease estrogen in the body: by avoiding environmental toxin xenoestrogens and by taking anti-estrogen supplements. Another way to balance out progesterone/estrogen levels, is by increasing progesterone. One way to do this is via progesterone creams.

Unfortunately, many modern "progesterone" creams are synthetically pharmaceutically produced. These artificially produced progesterone creams start off as natural progesterone but are then altered with chemicals so that the pharmaceutical companies can patent their formulas and make more money. These chemically altered progesterone creams are not recognized by the body in the same way that natural progesterone is. The chemicals also can have unpleasant side effects that normal, natural progesterone will not.

However, natural bio-identical progesterone cream, that the body will recognize, does exist. Natural bio-identical cream used to be very commonly prescribed in both the United States and the United Kingdom prior to the 1960's, when the pharmaceutical companies began produced artificial creams.

A good first step to take before beginning the use of progesterone cream is to get a hormone test done. This can easily be accomplished at home by acquiring a saliva hormone testing kit. You can either get these from a doctor, or order them online yourself, as they are relatively inexpensive.

With your hormone testing kit, you are going to want to test for estradiol (an estrogen hormone) and progesterone. Having an initial hormone test before you begin the progesterone cream treatment can give you a good idea of your baseline levels so you will know how much of an imbalance you have. It can also give you the ability to see how much the treatment affects you and your hormone levels.

There are several ways that estrogen dominance might present itself in your testing kit results. The first, and most typical imbalance is that of high estrogen and low progesterone. There is also high estrogen and normal progesterone, normal estrogen, and low progesterone, and both low estrogen and progesterone imbalances. It is also possible for the testing kit to show normal levels of estrogen and progesterone. If you are affected by endometriosis, however, it is highly likely that you do not have normal levels. Those affected by endometriosis will most likely have one of the types of imbalances listed above.

CBD &THC for Endometriosis:

CBD has certainly increased in popularity and public awareness in recent years. You can find it in almost everything from gummies to face creams. It has become a bit of a fad craze, but what is it exactly? Why is it so popular? Most people know that it is associated with the marijuana or cannabis plant, but do not actually know what CBD is.

CBD is short for cannabidiol, which is the second most prevalent active ingredient in the cannabis plant. Both marijuana and hemp plants are cannabis plants, the key difference is the THC levels. Marijuana cannabis plants have significantly higher levels of THC than hemp plants, which have very low levels of THC. Any cannabis plant with a THC content of 0.3% or less can be classified as hemp. If the plant has more than 0.3% THC content it is classified as marijuana.

THC, short for tetrahydrocannabinol, is the main psychoactive compound of cannabis, or the part that gets you "high" when smoking marijuana. When marijuana is smoked, THC is absorbed into the bloodstream and travels to the brain. There it attaches itself to the brain's naturally occurring cannabinoid receptors, which is known as the endocannabinoid system. The endocannabinoid system is located in the cerebral cortex, cerebellum and basal ganglia. These parts of the brain are responsible for thinking, memory, pleasure, coordination, and movement.[47]

It is possible to isolate the **CBD** compound from cannabis, or hemp plants, without THC, and to avoid any psychoactive effects. Essentially, taking CBD will not get you "high." Hemp and CBD oil are legal in all 50 states in the United States. Unlike medical marijuana, you do not need a prescription or medical card to purchase hemp or CBD either. Even though it is federally legal, some states however do haves stricter laws regarding production and sale, so it may be easier to find in some states than others.

CBD has become very popular as a health supplement and it purported to help with a variety of health issues. It really began to first gain notoriety when used as an anti-seizure treatment. In fact, the FDA recently approved the first ever CBD medicine for seizure conditions, Epidiolex. CBD has also been used with success for cancer patients, those suffering from anxiety, and those with chronic pain.

What about CBD for endometriosis? Recent research has actually shown that the health of the endocannabinoid system in the brain is closely linked to the health of the female reproductive system.[48] Having an imbalance in your endocannabinoid system could lead to problems with reproductive organs. It is believed that moderate use of phytocannabinoid supplements might be able to help balance the endocannabinoid system and help to treat conditions like endometriosis.

Cannabis has been used by women suffering from endometriosis and other reproductive health conditions since antiquity. In Ancient Mesopotamia, it was common for women to drink hemp beer when having troubles with menstruation. In Ancient Egypt, cannabis was sometimes applied vaginally. In Persia, ancient medical documents describe a preparation of juice from cannabis seeds put in the nostrils to treat migraines, calm uterine pains, and prevent miscarriage. In China, it was used for post-partum pain. A text from 16th century Vienna, Austria notes that ""Women stooping due to a disease of the uterus were said to stand up straight again after having inhaled the smoke of burning cannabis." In fact, cannabis was endorsed by many doctors in both the Eastern and Western World for many years. The personal physician to Queen Victoria, Sir John Russell Reynolds, prescribed the Queen monthly doses of cannabis to deal with menstrual discomfort. [49]

As we have discussed earlier, apoptosis, or your body's natural ability to destroy "bad" cells, is impaired in women suffering from endometriosis. The endocannabinoid system in the brain is actually linked to apoptosis and the body's ability to stop and regulate cell growth. This is why cannabinoids such as THC and CBD are sometimes used as a form of cancer treatment. The same principle applies to using CBD and an endometriosis treatment. Studies have shown that activating the endocannabinoid receptors, like can be done with CBD, can inhibit endometrial tissue from proliferating.[50]

Not only can CBD stop the proliferation of endometrial tissue, but it can also prevent endometrial cells from migrating outside of the uterus into other areas of the body.[51] As we have discussed before, this is a huge problem for many women with endometriosis. In fact, many women have issues with endometrial cells growth after surgical lesion removal, and sometimes even after full hysterectomy. Medicating with CBD could help stop this problem.

Both THC and CBD are known to inhibit vascularization (the process by which cells enter the vascular, or blood vessel system) of cancerous lesions.[52] More work still needs to be done on how this might apply to endometriosis, but some have inferred that it is likely it would have a similar effect. Endometriosis lesions can only grow and spread via the process of vascularization. Inhibiting that process should have the same result of stopping lesions proliferation.

Pain control is also a large aspect of endometriosis treatment, with which CBD and THC can help. In women with endometriosis, lesions can embed in abdominal tissue and aggravate the nerves, causing pain. CBD can interfere with innervation, or the stimulation of those nerves.[53]

CBD also is capable of desensitizing certain pain receptors, specifically TRPV1.[54] TRPV1 is the abbreviation for "transient receptor potential cation channel subfamily V member 1." TRPV1 is usually used by the body in situations that could be immediately harmful. It is especially good at quick reactions to extreme, damaging temperature changes. For example, say you accidentally touch a burning hot stove. Ouch! TRPV1 will tell you take your hand off. In that situation TRPV1 is super useful.

However, when it comes to chronic pain, TRPV1 is not so useful. When faced from inflammation endometriosis, your body releases chemicals that can increase the sensitivity of pain receptors like TRPV1. Unlike with the burning stove, you cannot just metaphorically "remove your hand." You already know you have endometriosis, feeling pain from it all the time is not useful. This is where CBD can come in and help you essentially "turn-off" that pain receptor by desensitizing TRPV1.

CBD can help to stop inflammation by helping to counteract an overactive immune system. Many CB2 receptors, part of your body's endocannabinoid system, are located in macrophages (your immune systems "killer cells"). When CB2 receptors are activated, they prevent macrophages from releasing proteins that cause inflammation. CBD and other cannabinoids are capable of activating CB2 receptors.[57] These anti-inflammation properties, combined with CBD's anti-pain properties, can help to control pain in the same way as many common off-the-shelf pain medications.

NSAIDs such as Ibuprofen are frequently prescribed for pain and inflammation caused by endometriosis. As we have discussed earlier though, they are not without their side effects, and long-term use can cause problems. Many women do not feel comfortable using NSAIDs on a regular basis. One of the reasons that NSAIDs can lead to gastrointestinal problems, one of the main side effects, is because they inhibit an enzyme called COX-1, which protests the stomach and intestinal linings. CBD acts on inflammation by inhibiting COX-2, not COX-1.

CBD is generally safe to take. It can have some side effects in some people, including dry mouth, diarrhea, reduced appetite, drowsiness, and fatigue. However, when compared to some other prescription medication the side effects are minimal. One thing to pay attention to when buying CBD products, is the quality of the product you are buying. Since CBD is relatively new on the market in a lot of products, due to prior illegality, not all CBD products are closely monitored or approved. Just like with other supplements you want to make sure the product is of good quality and does not have a lot of other unnecessary additives.

Another thing to consider when adding CBD to your treatment plan is if you are taking any other pharmaceuticals that it might interfere with. There are certain drugs that can interact with CBD, specifically those that are processed by cytochrome P450. [55, 56] One way to tell if you are taking a drug that is processed by cytochrome P450 is not eating grapefruit is also one of the recommendations while taking the drug. If you are taking one of these drugs, it does not mean CBD is off the table entirely, not all drugs processed by cytochrome P450 interact with CBD negatively. However, you should talk with your doctor before beginning CBD or cannabis supplementation.

CBD supplements are available in a variety of different forms. There are CBD oil products for topical application that are specifically designed to target women with endometriosis. There are also bath products, like Epsom salts with cannabis. Capsules and drinks with CBD are an option as well. Another CBD product that some women with endometriosis swear by, are cannabinoid infused vaginal suppositories. They claim the suppositories work incredibly well for endometriosis pain.

Many women with endometriosis have also turned to using products not only with CBD, but those containing the **THC** compound as well. THC is a cannabinoid just like CBD, so it has many of the same beneficial effects. However, unlike CBD, THC can activate a receptor that might potentially increase cell migration, which could lead to endometriosis spread. It is also suggested that using THC without the counterbalancing effects of CBD could lead to more long-term innervation, or aggravation of nerves. It is for this reason that some medical professionals suggest that women who are medicating with THC should not take it alone, and make sure to take it at the same time as CBD.

Medical marijuana has both CBD and THC, and more women are turning to medical marijuana prescriptions to ease endometriosis symptoms for a variety of reasons. Some women do want the psychoactive relaxation effect that comes with the THC. It can also lift your mood and help those that suffer from insomnia.

A 2020 study published in the *Journal of Obstetrics Gynaecology Canada* discovered that of one out of every eight Australian women with endometriosis, who use medical marijuana to treat their symptoms, rate cannabis as the most effective way they have found to manage their disorder. The women reported that the cannabis reduced their pain, nausea, gastrointestinal symptoms, insomnia, depression, and anxiety. They also reported that they experienced very few side effects. [58]

Smoking medical marijuana is a common method of consuming the drug. This is done both via vapor pens, and old-fashioned cigarettes. However, there are known risks to any kind of smoke inhalation, so ingesting the medical marijuana is also an option. There are several "edibles" companies that produce products specifically made for women dealing with endometriosis pain. There are also oral supplements in capsule and mouth spray forms available.

Not everyone is comfortable with the idea of using medical marijuana. If you want to use THC without significant psychoactive effects, it is possible to acquire lotions or other topical products containing both THC and CBD. However, not every state in the United States allows the use of medical marijuana or THC, so in some areas you will be limited to CBD use.

If you are interested in trying medical marijuana, it is obviously not without its side effects. They can include increased heart rate, dizziness, drowsiness, dry mouth, nausea, anxiety, increased appetite, impairment short-term memory, and euphoria. This article is not a recommendation to try cannabis. Not everyone will have the same reaction to cannabis. How cannabis medication will affect a person depends a lot on a variety of factors, not limited to size, weight, age, health, dosage, and tolerance. However, to receive a prescription, you will have to speak with a healthcare professional, so they should be able to advise you whether or not medical marijuana is the right choice for you.

Medicinal Mushrooms for Endometriosis:

When you hear the word "mushrooms" it is possible that you first think of one of two things, your average culinary mushrooms like portobellos or cremini mushrooms, or psychoactive "shrooms" which are generally Psilocybin containing mushrooms. When it comes to endometriosis treatment however, we are not referring to either of those types of mushrooms. "Medicinal mushrooms" are medically beneficial fungi that have high levels of compounds that are known to be healing. They have a multitude of health benefits, including boosting the immune system, containing antioxidants, having anti-inflammatory properties, helping regulate manage blood sugar, supporting brain health, supporting the nervous system, and giving increased energy and stamina.

Many women with endometriosis, who are taking a more holistic approach to their treatment, have incorporated medical mushrooms into their plan. Major byproducts of endometriosis that many women struggle with are fatigue and what is known as "endo brain fog."

"Endo brain fog" seriously affects many women with endometriosis, and it is commonly overlooked. Many suffering from it describe the condition as a combination of extreme fatigue and exhaustion, a constantly hazy mind, poor memory, and trouble focusing. Brain fog can seriously affect every aspect of your life. It can take away your energy and your cognitive ability to complete day-to-day tasks. It can make work difficult, and even socializing. People suffering from extreme brain fog might take twice as long completely a task that they normal would, they might forget what they are doing, they might even have trouble just holding a conversation. It can pose a huge difficultly to your ability to function in everyday society, and seriously impact your quality of life.

One mushroom that many women with endometriosis have tried to help combat brain fog and fatigue is **Lion's Mane**. Lion's Mane mushrooms, or *Hericium erinaceous*, are known primarily for their support of healthy brain function. They are rich in an important compound called beta-glucans. Beta-glucans are responsible for immune boosting antioxidants and neuro-protective chemicals. Beta-glucans help to protect against oxidative stress, which is closely tied to neurodegenerative disorders. In fact, Lion's Mane mushrooms have been used to help symptoms of Alzheimer's and Parkinson's disease.[61]

Lion's Mane grows on the trunks of hardwood trees in Northern forests. It has been used historically in Traditional Chinese Medicine to promote good cognitive function, and to help treat neurodegenerative conditions. Lion's Mane is excellent for helping with "brain fog" caused by endometriosis.

Lion's Mane is available in powdered supplement form, which can be added to food, or to your morning smoothie or coffee. It can also be consumed in a capsule form, or even cooked and eaten. Lion's Mane mushrooms are very tasty, and many people enjoyed eating them sauteed.

Another "mushroom" that can help women with endometriosis is **Chaga.** Firstly, Chaga, or *Inonotus Obliquus*, is not actually a mushroom. However, it is commonly considered a mushroom, so for the purposes of using it as a treatment, it is going to be included in this section on medicinal mushrooms. Chaga is actually a sclerotium. A sclerotium is hardened mass of fungal mycelium that grows on trees in the colder regions of the Northern Hemisphere, generally on birch trees. Since the sclerotium grows into the tree, there ends up being a combination of the fungal mycelium and the wood fiber in the final product. This is actually somewhat of an added bonus, because birch bark has many wonderful medicinal properties as well.

Traditionally, Chaga was used in Russia, beginning in the 16th century as a way of treating stomach ailments. Today it is believed to support immune function, liver health, brain health, increase longevity, and boot digestion. For those suffering from endometriosis Chaga can really help to ease gastrointestinal symptoms.[62] Studies have also shown that

Chaga can prevent the production of harmful cytokines which trigger inflammation.[63]

Chaga is generally consumed in a tea form, and drunk 2-3 times a week. It can generally be purchased either in a powder form, or in tea bags. It is also sold in tincture and extract form, which some people believe causes better absorption by the body.

Another energy boosting mushroom to help with fatigue from endometriosis is **Cordyceps**. Cordyceps is another mushroom used in Traditional Chinese Medicine and ancient Tibetan medicine. Cordyceps is prescribed by traditional healers to help with energy, appetite, stamina and endurance. [64] Cordyceps supplements typically come in powdered form and it is recommended that adults take approximately 1 tsp every day, for a long period of time.

Shitake mushrooms, or *Lentinula edodes*, are another kind of mushroom with surprising health benefits. Not only are they the most popular mushrooms in the world, but they are also packed full of B-vitamins which help control blood sugar levels and reduce inflammation in the body. They have long been used in Traditional Chinese Medicine, as well as a food source. Shitake mushrooms are quite delicious and are generally described as having a "meaty" flavor. They are incredibly versatile, and can be cooked in stir-fries, put in salads, boiled, roasted in the oven, and included in soups.

Known as the "mushroom of immortality" **Reishi** mushrooms, or *Ganoderma lingzhi*, have been in recorded use for at least 2000 years. It was historically used by Taoist monks in China to promote calmness, as well as aid with their meditation. It was also highly prized by Chinese Royalty, who believed it aided in longevity. Reishi mushrooms contain polysaccharides which boost immune function, as well as improving sleep, reducing stress, and helping with fatigue. [65]

It is recommended that Reishi be taken at least twice a day, to feel stress relieving effects and eliminate fatigue. Supplements are commonly made from a dried extract of the Reishi mushroom.

The **Maitake** mushroom means "dancing mushroom" in Japanese. It supposedly got its name, because its healing properties were so incredible, that people danced with joy when it was discovered. The mushroom grows at the bottom of Oak, Elm, and Maple trees, in the wild in parts of Japan, China, and North America. It is generally harvested in the autumn.

Maitake mushrooms are commonly used it recipes, and many people love the taste, but it is considered to be a medicinal mushroom. Maitake are a type of adaptogen. Adaptogens are herbs or mushrooms that have the unique ability to "adapt" their function to support the body's natural ability to deal with stress, which can vary. The specific needs that adaptogens can help with may be physical, chemical or biological. Maitake mushrooms generally also help with restoring normal insulin levels, which leads to less inflammation in the body.[66]

Emotional Healing:

Something that traditional medicine does not always consider is emotional health. Emotional and mental health are not separate from physical health and should not be viewed as such. The two are closely linked. Poor physical health can seriously affect your mental state. The reverse is also true: poor mental health has a direct affect and negative impact on your physical condition.

As was mentioned earlier, many women living with endometriosis also struggle with poor mental and emotional health, suffering from anxiety, depression and other problems. They also frequently exhibit somatization —the manifestation of physical symptoms due to emotional distress. The stress caused by chronic pain can lead to a somatic response, which physically harms the body. This can then cause increased endometriosis pain, which in turn increases stress levels. This perpetuates the vicious cycle of increasing stress and pain. This cycle can be very taxing on both the body and the mind.

Many women with endometriosis have suffered from chronic pain for essentially their entire adult lives. Sometimes they cannot even remember what it felt like to not be in pain. Living with such a condition can certainly feel profoundly unfair. Some women with endometriosis feel trapped in their own bodies, unable to live the lives they want to, because of their disease. They describe themselves as feeling alien. Having endometriosis is isolating. Those who do not suffer from endometriosis cannot ever truly understand the pain. It can be difficult to not fall into despair.

The stress and mental anguish of not being understood, and worse, not being believed, can certainly take a toll. Many women must fight to have their endometriosis diagnosis taken seriously. Endometriosis is not a disease that manifests in your outside appearance, so you can look perfectly fine on the outside, while internally you are suffering.

Unfortunately, while progress is being made, there is also still somewhat of a stigma against diseases related to reproductive health. Women can be embarrassed or ashamed to have to reveal they have endometriosis. Even if they do, they can be told that "it is not really that bad," and that "all women have period pain," because of a fundamental misunderstanding of the disease. Sometimes they might feel pressured into pushing themselves farther that they really should, physically and emotionally, at work, at home, and in relationships.

Many doctors in Western medicine also prescribe pharmaceuticals and other treatments without consideration for potential mental health effects. Medications, such as a hormonal birth control can have negative effects on the psyche. Many women, even those not suffering from endometriosis, experience increased depression and anxiety after taking hormonal birth control.

Surgery can also have similarly harmful effects on mental health. Many women experience severe emotional changes after receiving hysterectomies, something that is not often discussed. Reviews from the Mayo Clinic of patients that have undergone hysterectomies, showed that said patients have a 6.6% risk increase for depression and 4.7% risk increase for anxiety. Women who underwent hysterectomies at a younger than average age, between the ages of 18 and 35, the risk of depression was even higher, with a risk increase of 12%. [69]

As previously covered, neither hormonal birth control, nor surgery are cures for endometriosis, either. For many women, hormonal birth control and surgery are just not options. They are not willing to risk the harmful side effects for something that is not even guaranteed to help their condition. Especially for women that already suffered from clinical mental health issues such as depression and anxiety, the idea of disrupting your body and hormones even further is not a pleasant one.

This is where holistic healing can offer a better alternative. Holistic healing is not a band-aid to put on what can feel like the gaping wound of endometriosis. Holistic health practices try to look at the root causes of a problem, not just treat the symptoms. It also does not just target one aspect of health, or one part of the body and try to "fix" that part at the expense of the rest of your body, and your overall health.

When beginning your journey to holistic healing it is important first of all, to recognize that there is a connection between your physical and emotional health. Holistic health relies on treating and paying attention to your whole body. You must remember that your brain is just another organ. You must take care of it and treat it properly just like you would your heart, or lungs, or kidneys, or any other part of your body. Your mind and consciousness are also part of your body, they are what make you who you are. The wellbeing of your mind cannot be separated from the well-being of your body. We cannot treat our bodies like machines, isolated from any sort of feelings or emotions.

Self-observation and mindfulness:

To begin your journey to emotional healing, you must first become aware of where emotional distress lies and acknowledge it. Intentional self-observation and mindfulness can be hard to learn, but it is key to processing your emotions and healing.

Paying attention to yourself can seem counterintuitive. How can you avoid yourself? While it is true that we cannot avoid ourselves in the same sense we avoid other people, it is still very possible and very common for us to avoid certain parts of ourselves. Often, as a defense mechanism to try to avoid our own pain, we can close ourselves off and try to ignore suffering.

Learn to be present, and aware of your feelings. The first step is just to acknowledge your feelings. You do not have to take action against them yet, but even acknowledging them can be difficult. Even though it is bad for our mental health in the long run sometimes it can seem "easier" to bury things.

Take note of all the emotions you feel, good and bad. Try to notice when you feel positive emotions, and when you feel negative emotions. Pay attention to "triggers" for negative emotions. Sometimes triggers can be external stressors just as physical pain, or conflict with others. How do you know that negative emotions are being triggered? Here are some physical signs and manifestations:

- Sudden brain fog.
- Feeling like you are in "flight or fight mode."
- Increased heart rate.
- Unexplained nausea or stomach pains.
- Unreasonable anger or sadness.
- Muscle tension.
- Feeling jittery.
- Feeling "out of control."

Remember, a key part of mindfulness is to not judge yourself for your negative emotions. Take note of them, and accept them, but try to release any guilt associated with them. It is okay to not feel okay. You are not weak or less worthy because you feel negative emotions. Recognizing negative emotions and facing them, so that you might better yourself and improve your life, is one of the bravest things you can do.

Also pay attention to things that might cause positive emotions. Maybe you feel warm and cozy with a particular fuzzy blanket. Maybe exercise gave you a boost of endorphins. Maybe spending time with a loved one made you feel happy and appreciated. Keep track of the good feelings too, not just the bad ones.

Meditation:

Meditation is a type of mindfulness practice that is recorded to date back thousands of years. Almost every culture recognizes the benefits of meditation and has some sort of meditation practice. The word "meditation" in English originates in the word "meditatum", a Latin word meaning "to ponder."

In a 2019, in a study of Australian women with endometriosis, it was discovered that 47% used meditation as a form of self-management of their endometriosis.[70] A report from Psychology Today noted that "Imaging studies show that mindfulness soothes the brain patterns underlying pain and over time, these changes take root and alter the structure of the brain itself so that patients no longer feel pain with the same intensity."[71] Many women with endometriosis find this to be true, and find that meditation and mindfulness reduce their pain, anxiety, and "brain fog."

A common misconception of meditation is that it involves the complete clearing of your mind or thinking absolutely nothing. This is not true, in fact "clearing your mind" is not really possible. There are many different forms of mediation, but all of them involve mindfulness, careful awareness of oneself. Several different types of meditation are listed below:

Mindfulness meditation - mindfulness meditation originates from Buddhist teachings. It involves sitting still and silently, free of distractions, and simply paying attention to your thoughts as they pass through your mind. Remember not to judge your thoughts or emotions and try to not dwell on any one thing. Simply observe and take note of any patterns. Combine this concentration on your thought with awareness of your physical body. Pay special attention to your breath, and focus on taking full, deep breaths.

Religious or spiritual meditation - all major religions, including Hinduism, Buddhism, Judaism, Christianity, and Islam practice forms of meditation. Religious meditation is like prayer in that you focus your mind on speaking with or connecting with your God or deity, or if you are not particularly religious, with the Universe and life forces.

Focused meditation - focused meditation involves concentration using any of the five senses, sight, scent, touch, or sound. You can use anything from watching a lit flame, to smelling essential oils, or counting beads, or listening to music. Whatever you choose, try to focus all your attention on that one thing, and clear your mind of other distractions.

Movement meditation - movement meditation is any practice where you find peace and clarity in physical action and can let you mind wander. It can be anything from yoga, to tai chi, to walking, or gardening.

Mantra meditation - mantra meditation is common in many teachings that involve meditation, including Hindu and Buddhist traditions. Mantra meditation is the use of any repetitive sound or phrase to clear the mind. This can be anything from a simple "Om" to a repetitive prayer.

Visualization meditation - visualization meditation is a technique of meditation that focuses on visualizing certain scenes or images. You can choose to visualize a real place that you are familiar with. For example, somewhere that you feel calm and relaxed or you can create your own mental image. For example, some people like to visualize a garden and mentally "walk through" the garden. Other people use positive visualization to imagine their goal and future success.

Journaling:

Keeping a journal or diary is a wonderful way to monitor both your physical and emotional state when you have endometriosis. Bullet journaling can be a great way of simply keeping track of symptoms. Things to monitor include pain level, type of physical symptoms, daily mood, habits/self-care practices, and diet.

Freeform journaling can also help improve your mental health. Try to set aside just 15-20 minutes a day to write down whatever you are feeling. It does not have to follow any sort of special format, just let the words flow. Writing down all thoughts and feelings and externalizing those on to paper can help remove a load from your mind. It can also help you to better analyze and understand your emotions, from almost an outside perspective.

Gratitude journaling is another form of journaling that can help improve your outlook and help you to focus on the positive. You can either write a short paragraph of good things that happened during the day, or even something as simple as a "five things that I am thankful for" list. The idea is not to ignore or minimize your very present, and valid, challenges that come with endometriosis, but to help your brain refocus on the good for a little while.

For those that are more artistically inclined, visual journaling can also be soothing, and a helpful way of materializing emotions. You can keep an art journal, where you doodle or draw visual representations of how you are feeling. Many people find art therapy very helpful for coping with stress.

Therapy:

What better way to explore and learn to process your emotions than with a therapist, someone who is trained to help you? Pain-focused therapists are therapists that specifically work with patients that suffer from chronic pain and help them to sort through their accompanying emotions. They also provide support strategies for minimizing the effects stress can have on pain, and vice versa.

There are even therapists who specifically work with patients suffering from endometriosis as one of their specialties. Therapists that are trained in helping endometriosis patients can give you a safe, understanding, and judgement-free place to vent and deal with all the negative things that come along with the disease. It can also be incredibly helpful and validating to have someone to speak with that acknowledges your pain, when so frequently women with endometriosis can feel unheard.

Endometriosis can interfere with many aspects of your daily life such as work, exercise, hobbies, and relationships. Pain therapists can help you manage those difficulties and figure out ways to work around your pain and get back to living your life so you can avoid missing out.

Trauma Release Exercises:

Tension and Trauma Releasing Exercises (or TRE®) is a self-help tool that is designed to be learned and used independently as needed throughout a person's life. The idea is to continuously support and promote personal health and wellness, based on the principle that tension and trauma is both psychological and physical.

TRE® is a series of physical exercises that assists the body in releasing muscular stress, tension, and trauma. TRE® is essentially a response to the body's natural "fight or flight" reaction that can cause stress. The exercises performed activate the body's natural reflex mechanism of shaking that then releases muscular tension and calms down the nervous system. This activation allows the body to return to a state of balance and homeostasis and helps to purge stress.

There are TRE® resources and videos available online, as well as books and eBooks. It is also possible to get certified in the techniques, and there are providers who can guide you through the exercises and teach you how to implement them in your day-to-day life. The idea is to be able to practice and use the techniques for the rest of your life whenever needed, once you learn how to utilize them.

Reiki:

Reiki is a Japanese technique for stress reduction, relaxation, and healing. The word Reiki is composed of two Japanese words - Rei which means "God's Wisdom or the Higher Power" and Ki which means "life force energy." Essentially, when combined the word translates to "spiritually guided life force energy." Reiki is practiced by "laying on hands", focused on certain areas of energy, similarly to acupressure.

While spiritually connected, Reiki is not a religious practice, nor is it tied to any specific religion. It is performed over the clothes, and unlike acupressure does not involve any significant pressure. Instead, it is just light touching. Reiki is a simple, natural, and safe method of healing. Anyone can use it without any risks of side effects. It can also work when combined with other medical and therapeutic techniques.

Reiki can be learned and practiced by anyone. There are classes taught all over the world if you want to learn to practice Reiki on yourself or others. There are also professional practitioners of Reiki whom you can pay for a session.

Sound bath healing:

Sound bath healing is a practice similar to meditation. The goal of a sound bath session is to guide you into a deeply relaxed state while you are surrounded by ambient sound. This sound will be played by instructors, or sound therapists, and is generally created with traditional crystal bowls, gemstone bowls, cymbals, or gongs. The person undergoing the treatment will usually be seated or laying down on a comfortable cushion or mat.

Many studies point to the therapeutic effects of rhythmic sounds and music.[72] The sounds of the particular rhythmic vibrations that are created by the traditional instruments typically used in sound baths are intended to stimulate the alpha and theta brain waves. Alpha and theta brain waves are associated with deep meditative and peaceful states. It is thought that when we are able to access these states, then we are able to provide an environment in the body which is more conducive for healing. When your heart rate, respiratory rate, and breathing slows down this causes a therapeutic effect on the mind and body.

Coping with bad days:

As a person living with a chronic illness, it is inevitable that sometimes you will have a "bad day." A bad day can be a day where physical pain, or emotional distress, or both just seem to really knock you down. It might be impossible to get out of bed, or even if you do, daily tasks might seem miserable. It can be easy to fall into despair, so how do you deal with it?

(1) Remember that not every day will be this bad.

Some days it can be hard to feel like you are keeping your head above water. It can be absolutely overwhelming. You might just want to curl into yourself in misery. You might be overwhelmed by all the things you need to do that you feel incapable of. You might start catastrophizing and thinking: how is this ever going to get better? How am I ever going to get back on my feet and do the things I need to do? Just remember, tomorrow is a new day, and it has the potential to be better than the last.

It is okay to take a break, to retreat and rest. It is okay to set aside plans and tasks for another, better day. Do not try to push yourself. It is okay to watch tv, nap, or take a hot bath, or do any other number of "non-productive" things that help take your mind off the pain. Remember you are not being "lazy", you are taking care of yourself. Be easy on yourself.

(2) You do not have to act a certain way to "validate" your chronic illness.

Sometimes there will be good days. Days that you are not in much pain and you finally get to do the things you want to do and enjoy activities that you might not otherwise. To a person on the outside, who does not suffer from chronic illness and cannot "see" that you are ill, they might not understand. People can use this to misconstrue your illness or try to minimalize it. "If you can rollerblade, hike, dance, *insert literally any activity here*, then you must not be chronically ill!" They will say. Then, when you have a bad day they will say "Well you were just doing that activity the other day, it must not be that bad!" Obviously, this is not true. However, it can become incredibly frustrating.

It can also become easy to start questioning your own pain. You can start to wonder if maybe it is not really that bad, if maybe you are exaggerating. In reality, for a woman with endometriosis, it is quite the opposite. If the average person were suddenly struck with the kind of pain you endure daily, they would probably be completely incapacitated. Do the things you enjoy when you are capable of them. On the bad days, do whatever it is you need to do to make yourself as comfortable as possible. In the end, it does not matter what judgements other people may pass. Remember, you are incredibly strong, and you are worthy of happiness. Take advantage of your good days.

(3) Remember your illness does not define you.

You are not your disease, and neither is your body. Sometimes it can be easy to fall into the trap of hating your body, or feeling trapped in it, when you are suffering from chronic illness. Remember that your body is affected by your illness, and it is working hard to fight against it. Give your body, and yourself, some credit.

Sometimes when you experience so much suffering it can seem almost like a punishment. It can feel so profoundly unfair. Why me? Why do I deserve this? Just remember, your illness does not have any bearing on who you are as a person. In fact, as someone dealing with a chronic illness, you are stronger than most people can ever imagine. The fact that you are reading this booklet also means that you are trying to do everything you can to improve your life and your condition. That is the very definition of a fighter, and a warrior, and that is something of which to be very proud.

It can be easy to feel like you are being held back by your endometriosis, and feel discouraged, like you are not capable of "great things." Just remember that greatness is not always defined in the same ways. You do not have to save the world, sometimes the best thing you can do is fight for yourself. Just by getting up every day and continuing on, even in the face of horrible adversity, you are making the world a better place. Just by living, even when it is painful, you can encourage and help others that are also suffering. Every life, even a difficult one, is worth living.

(4) Do not apologize for being sick.

While your illness does not define you as a person, it *does* affect you. It fundamentally changes your lived experience, and that cannot be disregarded. You cannot be expected to live your life in the same way as a person not suffering from endometriosis. Other people do not have to fight to do daily tasks in the same way as a person suffering from chronic illness, and you should not be expected to push through everything.

If you must cancel plans, cancel them. If you need leeway in work or school, ask for help. If you need more support from family and friends, tell them. Never feel guilty for being affected by a disease that you have no control over. If someone expects you to push yourself beyond your limits, they do not respect you in the way that they should.

(5) Take time to recover and regroup.

The day after a "bad day" can be overwhelming. Start slowly, do not rush into doing everything that you were incapable of doing on your "bad day." Check in with yourself and your emotions. How are you feeling, are you feeling stressed? Exhausted? Sad? Anxious? Overwhelmed? Acknowledge your emotions and begin to process them. Take a deep breath and tell yourself it is going to be okay.

Sit down and make a list of the things you need to accomplish. Make it a short list. It is okay to save somethings for later. Do not try to push yourself too far, and trigger another "bad day." Continue to rest, and slowly reintegrate yourself into your normal routine. If your retreated and isolated yourself during your "bad day," reach out and reconnect. Contact the people you need to contact and explain the situation.

Finally, take action. Address the symptoms you were experiencing on your "bad day." If something triggered them, try to identify what that was. Reach out to your doctor or other medical professional. Try to assess the situation and do what you can to adjust.

Seeking support:

When you are suffering from a chronic illness you cannot power through alone, and you should not have to. You need people to talk to, people to help you when you are struggling, and people to comfort you when you are in pain. You need support.

Make sure you communicate with your family and loved ones. Often when you are chronically ill you can become use to saying "I'm fine" when you are really anything but fine. Sometimes it just seems easier. Explaining your pain can be exhausting. You might also feel like telling people the truth, that you are not fine, will burden them. To people that love you, and want the best for you, however, it is *not* a burden.

People that love you want to help you, you must give them the chance. On the other hand, remember that your friends and family are not mind readers. Tell them what you need. Tell them how they can help you. Specific requests are better. Do not just say "I am really struggling today." Say "I am really struggling today, could you walk the dog/do the laundry/wash the dishes for me? It would really help me out." Do not feel guilty for asking for help when you need it. If your loved ones asked you for help with something, would you be angry, or blame them for not being able to do it? Of course not.

Try to educate your friends and family members about your condition or encourage them to do their own research. Do not hide how much your disease affects you. Suffering from endometriosis is not something to be ashamed of, and it is not something you should have to keep hidden.

Sometimes women feel uncomfortable about having to explain a gynecological condition to friends or employers. Just remember, it is a chronic illness, and you deserve help and accommodation for it, just like any other condition. Your reproductive organs are just like any other part of your body! You would not feel ashamed to tell someone you had a heart condition, or a disability resulting from an injury, that required certain adjustments. Endometriosis is no different!

Try to find a doctor, counselor, or other medical professional that can be your advocate. There are also private patient or medical advocates that you can hire that specialize in helping patients and caregivers. Employers or schools should not discriminate against a person with a medical condition who is otherwise qualified and capable of performing essential functions. They also should provide reasonable accommodations. Many people are not very aware of what endometriosis is, or how severe symptoms can be. They might not understand the extent of your symptoms. Having a professional to back you up can be very helpful.

Reach out to others suffering from endometriosis. This can be someone you know who also has endometriosis, or you can see if there are any in-person support groups for women with endometriosis in your area. If not, you can also reach out through online forums and groups. Many women all over the world suffer from endometriosis. You are not alone!

Even if you have a supportive family and medical professionals, no one else who does not suffer from endometriosis can truly understand how you are feeling. It can be very isolating. However, there are others that are going through the same things you are and reaching out and finding an endometriosis "buddy" or group can make a world of difference. Sometimes you just need someone to talk and vent to that can understand.

"Endometriosis Association" was the first organization in the world created specifically for women with endometriosis. They are dedicated to endometriosis education, support, and research, and their resources can be found online. "My Endometriosis Team" is another resource which is a social network for women with endometriosis that has over 100,000 members. Talking with others suffering from endometriosis can give you emotional support and insights on managing the disease. Some women even form long-lasting friendships, a friend with whom they can share daily trials and successes when living with endometriosis.

Summary:

Hopefully reading this booklet has provided you with some insight into the condition of endometriosis and has provided you with some alternative options for treatment that are not commonly addressed by mainstream medicine. Endometriosis is an inflammatory, hormonal condition, to which there is no cure. Many treatments commonly prescribed by western doctors do not address the overall health and wellbeing of the person affected. Common treatments such as hormones or surgery only suppress or temporarily eliminate symptoms. They do not heal the body, or eliminate the disease, and all of them have significant risks.

Many women with endometriosis find that a holistic, full body approach to healing endometriosis, which addresses the root causes of the disease, is the most effective way of reducing pain and healing damage. Unlike pharmaceuticals, which have significant side effects after long term use, or surgery, which is a temporary fix, holistic treatment is possible to continue for one's whole life. Holistic treatment is, by definition, long-term and sustainable. The main goals of holistic therapy are to reduce inflammation and oxidative damage in the body, balance hormone levels, and optimize the body's natural detoxification processes.

Not only will a holistic health plan reduce the symptoms of your endometriosis, but it will improve your entire quality of life. Living a holistic lifestyle improves your mood, your physical abilities, your career, your relationships, and every other aspect of your life. Holistic health demonstrates a respect for your body and encourages a healthier worldview. Holistic treatments recognize the fact that all body systems are interconnected. Our mental, emotional, and physical health are all tied together, a fact which is not always recognized by traditional western medicine.

Know that there is hope, and there is an alternative way to what you have most likely been told before. You, and only you, are in control of your life and your treatment. There might not be a cure to endometriosis, but there is hope. Often conventional medicine and ideas about endometriosis leads us to believe that there is no end in sight, just a lifetime of pain and continuous symptoms. This could not be further from the truth.

Endometriosis might not be "curable," but it is certainly treatable. Many, many women find incredibly success with a variety of holistic health healing plans. It is possible to have endometriosis and live a normal life.

Endometriosis can be a challenging illness to tackle, but you do not have to accept pain as a way of life. The more you learn about the disease, and about holistic health treatments, the more tools you will have to fight back against endometriosis. Once you begin treating your whole body, and addressing the root causes of the disease, you may finally find solutions and relief from pain that you previously thought were impossible.

No one treatment plan for someone suffering from endometriosis will be the same. It is unlikely that every single idea or piece of advice included in this booklet will be right for you, and your circumstances. However, it can act as a good resource, and a starting point for your journey to health and holistic healing. Listed below are eight steps to take after reading this booklet:

(1) Take charge of your condition.

Realize that endometriosis is often poorly understood, even by medical professionals. Take time to research your condition. Try different approaches and research different treatments to find out what is best for you. Educate yourself and learn as much as you can about the condition. Read about other endometriosis sufferers experiences. Knowledge is power.

Do not wait to get help. Sometimes women wait to seek professional help for their endometriosis symptoms. A lot of times women might wonder if they really have endometriosis. They tell themselves maybe it is normal. Plenty of women have debilitating cramps, right? No, what you are experiencing is not normal. Being in excruciating pain is not normal, and you should not have to suffer through it.

Be assertive, and do not let others, even doctors, dismiss you. Be your own advocate. Remember that you have always have a right to say no. Just because a medical professional tells you that their opinion is the best option, whether that is a pill, or a surgery, or any other treatment, that does not mean you have to do it. Doctors and other health practitioners do not always know what is right for you. If something does not feel right, or you just do not feel comfortable with it, speak up. Seek a second opinion. Guide your own treatment.

(2) Realize Holistic Healing is a journey, not an instant fix.

Remember to pace yourself. It can be easy to get overly eager at the potential of healing your endometriosis. Do not start changing everything at once. Ease yourself into changes and integrate new treatments slowly. Especially when it comes to lifestyle changes, the more you try to implement at once, the less sustainable it will be. If you try to change too many things, you will burn out, and revert to previous behaviors.

Trying too many treatments at once will also prevent you from finding out what is really working and helping with your symptoms. Try one thing at a time, and give it a few weeks, or a few tries to determine how well it is working. If something works, like a diet change for example, keep doing it. Holistically healing your endometriosis is going to take fundamental changes to your way of life. It is going to require permanent change. This can be very difficult, but eventually you will adjust. Stick with it. It will be worth it in the end.

(3) Change your diet.

The main goal when changing your diet is to try to achieve as balanced a diet as possible. You want to receive the maximum amount of nutrients for the food you are consuming. Eat lots of healthy protein, fruits, and vegetables. Make sure you are getting all the necessary vitamins you need. Take supplements for those that you might be deficient in.

Focus on eating foods that are anti-inflammatory. These types of foods, which we have discussed, are not only not harmful, but can actually help ease your endometriosis. Try to incorporate as many as possible into your diet.

Eliminate "junk food" completely from your diet. It is okay to treat yourself but try to find healthier versions of foods that are really, truly bad for you. Try not to eat heavily fried food, or food packed full of artificial sugars, because it will lead to endometriosis flair ups.

Try to reduce or eliminate foods containing gluten. To see if you are sensitive to gluten, undergo an elimination diet. You must follow the two steps, and you cannot cheat, or the process will not work! Keep careful track of all your symptoms during first step, while you eliminate all forms of gluten. For the second step continue keeping careful track of your symptoms while you slowly start re-introducing healthy sources of gluten like whole wheat into your diet. Compare the symptoms from the two steps. If you have a significant increase of symptoms during the second, re-introduction period, it is most likely a good idea to adopt a healthy, permanently gluten-free diet.

Try to reduce or eliminate foods with high levels of estrogen. High estrogen foods are known to make endometriosis symptoms worse. Avoid soy products, and non-organic red meat and dairy, all of which can increase estrogen levels in the body.

(4) Change your lifestyle.

Try to eliminate alcohol, coffee, and smoking from your lifestyle. Get enough sleep. Make sure you stay hydrated. Try to reduce the harm to your body as much as possible. Do not do things that will actively work against your healing journey.

Stay active, but do not push it. When it comes to exercise, listen to your body. Over exercising and overexerting yourself can exacerbate endometriosis symptoms. When done correctly however, exercise can improve symptoms significantly. Exercise improves blood flood, releases endorphins, and lowers estrogen.

Try to reduce your stress as much as possible. Stress hurts your body and impedes your healing. It can also make you more sensitive to pain. Try calming exercises such as yoga or walking to reduce stress levels. You can also try taking supplements or practicing some of the stress reduction techniques we have covered.

(5) Avoid environmental toxins.

As we have talked about, modern humans are exposed to a ridiculous amount of environmental toxins almost daily. Check all of the products you use around your home and replace them with toxin-free alternatives. Making your own cleaning and household products can save you money in addition to eliminating the toxins in your home.

Eliminate your plastic use as a much as possible. Get a metal or glass water bottle. Try to use ceramic or glass containers for cooking and food storage as much as possible. Never heat up anything in plastic. Filter your water. Eat organic food as much as possible. Buy hormone-free meat.

Make sure you only use toxin-free beauty products and feminine hygiene products. Anything that is coming into direct contact with your skin has the potential to transfer lots of toxins and estrogen-mimickers into your body.

(6) Test for and treat hormone imbalances.

We know endometriosis is an estrogen dominant condition. If you are suffering from endometriosis it is likely you have an imbalance between your progesterone and estrogen. Most likely you have too much estrogen, and too little progesterone. Testing for hormone imbalances is a good first step. Once you identify the exact type of imbalance you have you can start to try to correct it.

As we have discussed, avoiding environmental toxins, as well as eliminating foods that are high in estrogen is key. Increase progesterone levels can also help, such as by using progesterone creams like was covered earlier.

(7) Pursue alternative treatments and remedies.

Hormonal therapies and surgeries are not your only options for treatment and relief from endometriosis symptoms. Other than holistic medicines, foods, and lifestyles changes, there are also the forms of non-invasive therapies and pain relief that we have covered in this booklet, as well as many more. Do research and try different things to see what works for you.

(8) Be kind to yourself and your body.

Try to catch yourself when you begin thinking negative thoughts. If you start thinking things like "maybe if I just tried harder," or "maybe I am exaggerating my pain," or "I should be able to do this," just stop, and take a breath. Clear your mind and try to think what you would say to a friend who was in the same situation. Would be as hard on someone you love as you are being on yourself? Probably not, right? You would tell them that they are strong, and that they are doing to the best that they can. You would tell them that they need to be kind to themselves.

Grant yourself the same forgiveness and understanding. You understand your body better than anyone else, do not push it beyond what it is capable of. Trying to overextend yourself, physically or mentally, will just end up backfiring. Healing from endometriosis is a journey. It can be a long and difficult one, but do not give up hope. Keep fighting for yourself. You are worthy and you can do this!

Citations

1) Mehedintu, C., Plotogea M.N., Ionescu, S., & Antonovici, M. (2014). Endometriosis still a challenge. *J Med Life, 7*(3): 349–357.

2) Ricciotti, E., & Fitzgerald, G.A. (2011). Prostaglandins and Inflammation. Arterioscler Thromb Vasc Biol, 31(5): 986–1000.

3) Mitchell, M.D. (1981). Prostaglandins during pregnancy and the perinatal period. Reproduction, 62: 305-315.

4) Lemaire, G. (2004). More than just menstrual cramps: symptoms and uncertainty among women with endometriosis. *Clinical Research, 33*(1): 71-79.

5) Laganà, A. S., et. al. (2017). Anxiety and depression in patients with endometriosis: impact and management challenges. *International Journal of Women's Health, 9*: 323–330.

6) Nnoaham, K.E., et al. (2011). Impact of endometriosis on quality of life and work

productivity: a multicenter study across ten countries. *Fertility and Sterility, 96*(2): 366-373.
7) Acién, P., & Velasco, I. (2013). Endometriosis: A Disease That Remains Enigmatic. *International Scholarly Research Notices.* Article ID 242149, 12 pages.
8) Nezhat, C., Nezhat, F., & Nezhat, C. (2012). Endometriosis: ancient disease, ancient treatments. *Fertility and sterility, 98*(6): S1-S62.
9) What causes endometriosis? *Endometriosis Foundation of America.* https://www.endofound.org/what-causes-endometriosis#:~:text=Stem%20cell%20theory%20posits%20that,endometrial%20cells%20and%20cause%20endometriosis. Accessed 9/05/2020.
10) Bellelis P., Podgaec S., & Abrão M.S. (1992). Environmental factors and endometriosis. *Rev Assoc Med Bras, 57*(4):448-452.
11) Hysterectomy. 2019. Office on Women's Health: U.S. *Department of Health and Human Services.* https://www.womenshealth.gov/a-z-topics/hysterectomy#:~:text=Each%20year%20in%20the%20United%20States%2C%20nearly%20500%2C000%20women%20get%20hysterectomies.&text=A%20hysterectomy%20is%20the%20second,delivery%20(C%2Dsection). Accessed 9/06/2020.

12) Fung, T., Rimm, E., Spiegelman, D., Rifai, N. Tofler, G., Willett, W., & Hu, F. (2001). Association between dietary patterns and plasma biomarkers of obesity and cardiovascular disease risk. *The American Journal of Clinical Nutrition, 73*(1): 61–7.
13) Stöppler, M. What Is the Definition of Organic Food? *MedicineNet.* https://www.medicinenet.com/what_is_the_definiti on_of_organic_food/views.htm Accessed 9/10/2020.
14) Yeung, P., Catanzaro, R. The Anti Inflammatory and Elimination Diet for Adults Living with Endometriosis. *Saint Louis University School of Medicine Department of Obstetrics, Gynecology, and Women's Health Center for Endometriosis.*
15) Harris, H.R., Eke, A.C., Chavarro, J.E., Missmer S.A. (2018). Fruit and vegetable consumption and risk of endometriosis. *Human Reproduction, 33*(4): 715–727.
16) Simmen, R., & Kelley, A. S. (2018). Seeing red: diet and endometriosis risk. *Annals of Translational Medicine. 6*(2), S119. https://doi.org/10.21037/atm.2018.12.14
17) Tsuchiya, M., Miura, T., Hanaoka, T., et al. (2007). Effect of soy isoflavones on endometriosis: interaction with estrogen receptor 2 gene polymorphism. *Epidemiology. 18*(3):402-408.

18) Santanam, N., Kavtaradze, N., Murphy, A., Dominguez, C., Parthasarathy, S. (2012). Antioxidant supplementation reduces endometriosis-related pelvic pain in humans. *Transl Res, 161*(3):189-195.
19) Pavone, M. E., Malpani, S. S., Dyson, M., Kim, J. J., & Bulun, S. E. (2016). Fenretinide: a potential treatment for endometriosis. *Reproductive Sciences, 23*(9), 1139-1147.
20) Acupuncture and Herbs Ameliorate Endometriosis. 2017. *HealthCMi.* https://www.nccaom.org/wp-content/uploads/pdf/Acupuncture%20And%20Herbs%20Ameliorate%20Endometriosis.pdf Accessed 09/30/2020.
21) Xiang D, Situ Y, Liang X, Cheng L, Zhang G. (2002). Ear acupuncture therapy for 37 cases of dysmenorrhea due to endometriosis. *J Tradit Chin Med, 22*(4):282-5. PMID: 16579094.
22) Zhu X, Hamilton KD, McNicol ED. (2011). Acupuncture for pain in endometriosis. *Cochrane Database Syst Rev*, 9:CD007864. doi:10.1002/14651858.CD007864.pub2 PMID: 21901713.
23) Lewis, I. (2020). How Can QiGong Help With Endometriosis? *Endo360Help.* https://www.endo360help.com/blog/how-can-

qigong-help-with-endometriosis/ Accessed 10/10/2020.
24) Fang, Ruei-Chi et al. (2012). "The traditional chinese medicine prescription pattern of endometriosis patients in taiwan: a population-based study." *Evidence-based complementary and alternative medicine.* doi:10.1155/2012/591391
25) Awad, Eman et al. (2017). "Efficacy of exercise on pelvic pain and posture associated with endometriosis: within subject design." *Journal of Physical Therapy Science, 29*,12: 2112-2115.
26) Genevive R. Meredith, et. al. (2020). Minimum Time Dose in Nature to Positively Impact the Mental Health of College-Aged Students, and How to Measure It: A Scoping Review. *Frontiers in Psychology.* doi:10.3389/fpsyg.2019.02942
27) Massart F., et. al. (2006). How do environmental estrogen disruptors induce precocious puberty? *Minerva Pediatr, 58*(3):247-54.
28) Korsunsky, D. (2020). The Science of Saunas: 10 Proven Clinical Health Benefits. *Heads Up Health.* https://headsuphealth.com/blog/features/benefits-of-saunas/ Accessed 10/19/2020.
29) Henke F. (2000). Alternative Hautpflege: Fit und vital durch Trockenbürsten [Alternative skin care: fit and

revitalized with the aid of dry brushing]. *Pflege Z.*, *53*(2):95-6. German. PMID: 10797750.

30) Battalangio, B. (2018). What Is a Colonic and Should You Get One? *Healthy Woman.* https://www.healthywomen.org/your-health/your-body/what-colonic-and-should-you-get-one. Accessed 10/20/2020.

31) Jain, N.K., Patel, V.P., Pitchumoni, C.S. (1986). Efficacy of activated charcoal in reducing intestinal gas: a double-blind clinical trial. *Am J Gastroenterol*, *81*(7):532-5. PMID: 3521259.

32) Hausswirth C, Louis J, Bieuzen F, Pournot H, Fournier J, et al. (2011). Effects of Whole-Body Cryotherapy vs. Far-Infrared vs. Passive Modalities on Recovery from Exercise-Induced Muscle Damage in Highly-Trained Runners. *PLOS ONE, 6*(12): e27749. https://doi.org/10.1371/journal.pone.0027749

33) Mattson, M. P., Longo, V. D., & Harvie, M. (2017). Impact of intermittent fasting on health and disease processes. *Ageing research reviews, 39*, 46-58.

34) Mahoney, E. How does an Ionic Foot Bath work? *Sacred Roots Holistic Healing.* https://sacredrootsholistichealing.com/benefits-ionic-foot-bath/ Accessed 10/20/2020

35) Sullivan, D. (2019). How to Make and Use Castor Oil Packs. *Healthline.* https://www.healthline.com/health/castor-oil-pack#takeaway Accessed 10/21/2020

36) Whitworth, G. (2020). The What, Why, and How of Epsom Salt Baths. *Healthline.* https://www.healthline.com/health/epsom-salt-bath. Accessed 10/21/2020

37) Leech, J. (2018). 10 Health Benefits of Spirulina. *Healthline.* https://www.healthline.com/nutrition/10-proven-benefits-of-spirulina#TOC_TITLE_HDR_4. Accessed 10/24/2020.

38) Mira T, et al. (2015). Effectiveness of complementary pain treatment for women with deep endometriosis through Transcutaneous Electrical Nerve Stimulation (TENS): randomized controlled trial. *Eur J Obstet Gynecol Reprod Biol, 194*: 1-6.

39) Behbahani, B.M. et al. (2016). "Comparison of the effects of acupressure and self-care behaviors training on the intensity of primary dysmenorrhea based on McGill pain questionnaire among Shiraz University students." *Journal of Research in Medical Sciences : The Official Journal of Isfahan University of Medical Sciences, 21*: 104. 2.

40) Narvekar, et al. (2004). "Low-dose mifepristone inhibits endometrial proliferation and up-regulates androgen receptor." *The Journal of Clinical Endocrinology & Metabolism. 89*:5: 2491-2497.

41) Hao, M., Zhao, W.H., Wang Y.H. (2009). Correlation between pelvic adhesions and pain symptoms of endometriosis. *Zhonghua Fu Chan Ke Za Zhi. 44*(5):333-6.

42) Marzin, T., et al. (2017). Effects of a systemic enzyme therapy in healthy active adults after exhaustive eccentric exercise: A randomised, two-stage, double-blinded, placebo-controlled trial. *BMJ Open Sport & Exercise Medicine, 2*: 1 e000191 doi:10.1136/bmjsem-2016-000191

43) Chen, H. et al. (2018). Nattokinase: A Promising Alternative in Prevention and Treatment of Cardiovascular Diseases. *Biomarker Insights, 13.* 1177271918785130 doi:10.1177/1177271918785130

44) Varayil, J. E., Bauer, B. A., & Hurt, R. T. (2014). Over-the-counter enzyme supplements: what a clinician needs to know. *In Mayo Clinic Proceedings, 89*(9): 1307-1312.

45) Pavone, M.E., & Bulun, S.R. (2013). The Use of Aromatase Inhibitors for Ovulation Induction and Superovulation. *The Journal of Clinical Endocrinology &*

Metabolism, 98(5) 1:1838–1844.
https://doi.org/10.1210/jc.2013-1328

46) Gonzales, G. F. (2012). Ethnobiology and Ethnopharmacology of Lepidium meyenii(Maca), a Plant from the Peruvian Highlands. *Evidence-Based Complementary and Alternative Medicine.* 1–10. doi: 10.1155/2012/193496

47) Elphick, M.R., & Egertová, M. (2001). The neurobiology and evolution of cannabinoid signalling. *Philosophical Transactions of the Royal Society B: Biological Sciences, 356*(1407): 381–408. doi:10.1098/rstb.2000.0787.

48) Di Blasio, A., Vignali, M., & Gentilini, D. (2013). The endocannabinoid pathway and the female reproductive organs. *Journal of Molecular Endocrinology, 50*(1), R1-R9.

49) Russo, E. (2002). Cannabis Treatments in Obstetrics and Gynecology: A Historical Review. *J Cannabis Therapeut, 2.* 5-35.

50) Leconte, M., et. al. (2010). Antiproliferative Effects of Cannabinoid Agonists on Deep Infiltrating Endometriosis. *The American Journal of Pathology, 177*(6) 2963-2970.

51) McHugh, D., Page, J., Dunn, E. & Bradshaw, H.B. (2012). Δ9-Tetrahydrocannabinol and N-arachidonyl

glycine are full agonists at GPR18 receptors and induce migration in human endometrial HEC-1B cells. *British Journal of Pharmacology, 165*(8) 2414-2424.

52) Freimuth, N., Ramer, R. & Hinz, B. 2010. Antitumorigenic effects of cannabinoids beyond apoptosis. *Journal of Pharmacology and Experimental Therapeutics, 332*(2) 336-344.

53) Hongxiu H. et. al. (2017). Cannabinoid receptor 1 contributes to sprouted innervation in endometrial ectopic growth through mitogen-activated protein kinase activation. *Brain Research.* (1663)132-140.

54) Iannotti F.A, et. al. (2014). Nonpsychotropic Plant Cannabinoids, Cannabidivarin (CBDV) and Cannabidiol (CBD), Activate and Desensitize Transient Receptor Potential Vanilloid 1 (TRPV1) Channels in Vitro: Potential for the Treatment of Neuronal Hyperexcitability. *ACS Chemical Neuroscience, 5*(11) 1131-1141.

55) Yamaori, S., et. al. (2011). Potent inhibition of human cytochrome P450 3A isoforms by cannabidiol: Role of phenolic hydroxyl groups in the resorcinol moiety. *Life Sciences,* (88): 15–16.

56) Devvit-Lee, A. (2018). CBD-Drug Interactions: Role of Cytochrome P450. *Project CBD.*

https://www.projectcbd.org/medicine/cbd-drug-interactions/p450 Accessed 11/18/2020.

57) Bouaziz, J., et. al. (2017). The Clinical Significance of Endocannabinoids in Endometriosis Pain Management. *Cannabis and Cannabinoid Research.* (December) 72-80.
http://doi.org/10.1089/can.2016.0035

58) Sinclair, J., Smith, C.A., Abbott, J., Chalmers, K.J., Pate, D.W. & Armour, M. (2020). Cannabis use, a self-management strategy among Australian women with endometriosis: results from a national online survey. *Journal of Obstetrics and Gynaecology Canada, 42*(3) 256-261.

59) Horne, A. W., Brown, J. K., Nio-Kobayashi, J., Abidin, H. B., Adin, Z. E., Boswell, L., Burgess, S., Lee, K. F., & Duncan, W. C. (2014). The association between smoking and ectopic pregnancy: Why nicotine is BAD for your fallopian tube. *PloS one, 9*(2), e89400.
https://doi.org/10.1371/journal.pone.0089400

60) Saraswat, L., et al. (2015). Reproductive and pregnancy outcomes in women with endometriosis: A Scottish national record linkage study. *ESHRE2015* Abstract O-122.

61) Friedman, M. (2015). Chemistry, nutrition, and health-promoting properties of Hericium erinaceus (lion's mane) mushroom fruiting bodies and mycelia and their bioactive compounds. *Journal of Agricultural and Food Chemistry*, 63(32) 7108-7123.
62) Shashkina, M.Y., Shashkin, P.N. & Sergeev, A.V. (2006). Chemical and medicobiological properties of chaga (review). *Pharm Chem J*, 40, 560–568
63) Kim, Y. R. (2005). Immunomodulatory Activity of the Water Extract from Medicinal Mushroom Inonotus obliquus. *Mycobiology, 33*(3), 158–162.
64) Panda, A. K., & Swain, K. C. (2011). Traditional uses and medicinal potential of Cordyceps sinensis of Sikkim. *Journal of Ayurveda and Integrative Medicine, 2*(1), 9–13.
65) Wachtel-Galor, S., et al. Ganoderma lucidum (Lingzhi or Reishi): A Medicinal Mushroom. In: *Benzie IFF, Wachtel-Galor S, editors. Herbal Medicine: Biomolecular and Clinical Aspects. (2nd ed.).* Boca Raton (FL): CRC Press/Taylor & Francis; 2011. Chapter 9. Available from: https://www.ncbi.nlm.nih.gov/books/NBK92757/
66) Lull, C., Wichers, H. J., & Savelkoul, H. F. (2005). Antinflammatory and immunomodulating properties

of fungal metabolites. *Mediators of Inflammation. 2005*(2), 63–80.

67) Wurn, B., Wurn, L., Patterson, K., King, R., & Scharf, E. (2011). Decreasing dyspareunia and dysmenorrhea in women with endometriosis via a manual physical therapy: Results from two independent studies. *Journal of Endometriosis 3*, 188-196.

68) Rajoria, S., et al. (2011). 3,3'-diindolylmethane modulates estrogen metabolism in patients with thyroid proliferative disease: a pilot study. *Thyroid: Official Journal of the American Thyroid Association, 21*(3): 299-304.

69) Furst, J. (2019). Study finds women at greater risk of depression, anxiety after hysterectomy. *Mayo Clinic.* https://newsnetwork.mayoclinic.org/discussion/study-finds-women-at-greater-risk-of-depression-anxiety-after-hysterectomy/. Accessed 11/20/2020.

70) Armour, M., et al. (2019). Self-management strategies amongst Australian women with endometriosis: a national online survey. *BMC Complementary and Alternative Medicine, 19*(1)17.

71) Penman, D. (2015). Can Mindfulness Meditation Really Reduce Pain and Suffering? *Psychology Today.* https://www.psychologytoday.com/intl/blog/mindf

ulness-in-frantic-world/201501/can-mindfulness-meditation-really-reduce-pain-and-suffering#comments_bottom Accessed 10/20/2020.

72) Saarman, E. (2016). Feeling the beat: Symposium explores the therapeutic effects of rhythmic music. *Stanford Report*. https://news.stanford.edu/news/2006/may31/brainwave-053106.html Accessed 11/28/2020.

www.ingramcontent.com/pod-product-compliance
Lightning Source LLC
Chambersburg PA
CBHW071446070526
44578CB00001B/224